Praise for
Awakening to the Secret Code of Your Mind

"The techniques shared in this book are age-old and have survived because they are productive. By using them, you can become empowered to find peace, love, and healing in your life. When you find peace in your life and create it in the world, the result will be what we all desire for ourselves and humankind."

— **Bernie S. Siegel, M.D.**, the best-selling author of
365 Prescriptions for the Soul and *Faith, Hope & Healing*

"Building upon the latest in mind-body research, Darren Weissman's 'Infinite Love & Gratitude' process reveals how we can quickly access and reprogram limiting beliefs that undermine our health and behavior. Dr Weissman offers readers of **Awakening to the Secret Code of Your Mind** *empowering insights that free us from self-sabotaging stories and emotions so that we may create the positive futures we desire."*

— **Bruce H. Lipton, Ph.D.**, the best-selling author of
The Biology of Belief and co-author of *Spontaneous Evolution*

"Everything about **Awakening to the Secret Code of Your Mind** *brings healing. Darren Weissman's The LifeLine Technique will shift how you approach your physical, mental, emotional, and even financial issues. This truly empowering and inspiring book will change your life forever."*

— **Sandra Anne Taylor**, the best-selling author of
Quantum Success and *Secrets of Attraction*

"Having personally experienced Dr. Darren Weissman's LifeLine Technique, I can attest that his system will enable you to harness the power of Infinite Love & Gratitude to create lasting and positive change. His new book is a step-by-step guide to total life transformation—empowering you to heal yourself physically, emotionally, and spiritually—for the rest of your life."

— **Denise Marek**, the best-selling author of
CALM and co-author of *The Keys*

"Dr. Darren Weissman shows you the way to achieve a life of authenticity and well-being and spread Infinite Love & Gratitude from the inside out. A true healer, he shares words that resonate with honesty, integrity, and compassion. The Lifeline Technique works if you're willing to spend a little time to explore the wonders of you! I highly recommend this book."

— **Colette Baron-Reid**, the best-selling author of
Messages from Spirit and *Remembering the Future*

"Having worked in natural health for decades, I have seen how subconscious suppressed emotions can limit people's ability to heal. The LifeLine Technique is a fast, effective healing modality that allows you to release subconscious emotions that are holding you back. In Dr. Weissman's new book, **Awakening to the Secret Code of Your Mind**, you learn how to do The LifeLine Technique for yourself, a gift to take your healing—and your life—to a whole new level."

— **Donna Gates**, the best-selling author of *The Body Ecology Diet*

"Truly an amazing book! I highly recommend it to anyone who is sincerely interested in changing themselves, and in the course of doing so, changing the world. Dr. Darren Weissman has done it again by creating a book that is rich with life-altering stories and that teaches you The LifeLine Technique, which can be experienced anywhere, anytime, and by anyone—with powerful results."

— **Carol Ritberger, Ph.D.**, the best-selling author of *Healing Happens with Your Help* and *What Color Is Your Personality?*

"Dr. Weissman has been a good friend of mine since I met him at a Hay House 'I Can Do It!' conference in Toronto. He has a pure heart, and I can be healed just staying beside him. He remotely sent me healing energy using The LifeLine Technique when I suffered from gangrene of my foot two years ago, and I had an amazing recovery after that! As a person who experienced his healing, I would like to recommend this book for you."

— **Masaru Emoto**, the best-selling author of *Messages from Water* and *The Healing Power of Water*

"In *Awakening to the Secret Code of Your Mind*, Dr. Darren Weissman provides you with the tools to transform your life using The LifeLine Technique. The positive results will astound you!"

— **Peggy McColl**, the best-selling author of *Your Destiny Switch* and *The Won Thing*

"Darren helps people uncover the unconscious patterns sabotaging their lives and use their own love to liberate the person they were born to be. This book is a groundbreaking road map for transforming your life and inducing change out in the world."

— **Lauren Mackler**, the best-selling author of *Solemate*

"Reading this book will help you connect more consciously with yourself and the Great Soul of the Universe. It is both inspirational and practical."

— **Tim** and **Kris Hallbom**, the founders of the NLP Institute of California

"The techniques shared in this book are a gift at many levels, and have the added advantage of providing you with one of life's rare no-nonsense opportunities. Worst case, you get to experience Infinite Love & Gratitude; best case, you get to experience Infinite Love & Gratitude while your body heals and your life improves beyond measure!"

— **Michael Neill**, the best-selling author of *You Can Have What You Want*, and founder of Supercoach Academy

Awakening
to the
Secret Code
of Your
Mind

Also by Dr. Darren R. Weissman

Contributing author to
THE HEALING POWER OF WATER,
by Masaru Emoto*

HEALTHY PROFITS:
The 5 Elements of Strategic Wellness in The Workplace,
by Sandra Larkin (contributing author)

THE POWER OF INFINITE LOVE & GRATITUDE:
An Evolutionary Journey to Awakening Your Spirit*

⊕ ⊕ ⊕

*Available from Hay House

Please visit Hay House USA: **www.hayhouse.com**®
Hay House Australia: **www.hayhouse.com.au**
Hay House UK: **www.hayhouse.co.uk**
Hay House South Africa: **www.hayhouse.co.za**
Hay House India: **www.hayhouse.co.in**

AWAKENING TO THE SECRET CODE OF YOUR MIND

Your Mind's Journey to Inner Peace

Dr. Darren R. Weissman

HAY HOUSE, INC.
Carlsbad, California • New York City
London • Sydney • Johannesburg
Vancouver • Hong Kong • New Delhi

Published and distributed in the United States by: Hay House, Inc.: www.hayhouse
.com • *Published and distributed in Australia by:* Hay House Australia Pty. Ltd.:
www.hayhouse.com.au • *Published and distributed in the United Kingdom by:*
Hay House UK, Ltd.: www.hayhouse.co.uk • *Published and distributed in the
Republic of South Africa by:* Hay House SA (Pty), Ltd.: www.hayhouse.co.za •
Distributed in Canada by: Raincoast: www.raincoast.com • *Published in India
by:* Hay House Publishers India: www.hayhouse.co.in

Design: Jami Goddess • *Interior photos:* Nicole Thomas: **www.nicolethomas.com**
Indexer: Joan Shapiro

Reprinted with permission: The LifeLine Technique™ Training Program materials,
with permission of Infinite Love Press, Inc. Copyright © 2002. All rights reserved.

Library of Congress Cataloging-in-Publication Data

Weissman, Darren R.
 Awakening to the secret code of your mind : your mind's journey to inner peace
/ Darren R. Weissman.
   p. cm.
 Includes index.
 ISBN 978-1-4019-2383-9 (tradepaper : alk. paper) 1. Mind and body. 2. Self-
perception. 3. Self-actualization (Psychology) 4. Subconsciousness. I. Title.
 BF161.W39 2010
 158--dc22

                                    2009043290

ISBN: 978-1-4019-2383-9

13 12 11 10   5 4 3 2
1st edition, March 2010
2nd edition, March 2010

Printed in the United States of America

For my beautiful and treasured wife, Sarit;
and for the future of our children:
Joya Ruth
Rumi Neve
Liam Yale

Contents

Foreword

On February 28, 1953, Francis Crick, the co-discoverer of the DNA molecule, bolted into The Eagle pub in Cambridge, England, and proclaimed that he and his colleague James Watson had solved one of the greatest mysteries of human existence. "We have found the secret of life!" those in the pub remember him saying. And with that proclamation, the human species began a new era in understanding ourselves and our relationship to our world. The rest, as they say, is history.

And while the discovery of the DNA molecule itself is, without a doubt, a pivotal event in the quest to know ourselves, it also opened the door to an even greater possibility, with even greater implications—the possibility of an intelligent design that forms the core of our existence.

When Watson, Crick, and others in the scientific community first recognized the pattern of the DNA molecule, they were immediately struck by its beauty, elegance, and simplicity. And as scientists, they couldn't deny its unmistakable order. That such a molecule can exist, sustain itself, correct/heal the errors that it finds within itself, and perpetuate itself for millions of years suggests that some kind of cosmic blueprint is involved. And for some people, these undeniable facts imply that DNA is intentional—that something, or someone, created the code of life.

While there are many theories and much speculation, the fact is that we simply don't know for certain how DNA originated or why it showed up on Earth. And although we could search for another 100 years and still not answer these questions, we must acknowledge what we do know. It's a fact that the odds in favor of DNA forming purely by chance are astronomically small.

It's precisely *because* the code of life appears to reflect some grand design that it also makes perfect sense that the code would come with instructions for its use— techniques that we can know, teach, and share. And that's where *this* book comes in.

A growing body of scientific evidence now suggests that the language to choose healing, longevity, peace, and even life itself also exists as a code. More precisely, it appears to be a code within a code. Just the way the letters on a keyboard (a code) command the unseen electronics (another code) of a computer, cell phone, or PDA, it appears that we are born with the ability to create the conditions for our DNA to thrive, exist, or wither. Unlike the DNA code, however, the language to operate our lives is not found as a linear sequence of instructions. It's not the kind of code that we can translate as sentences onto a piece of paper or a computer screen.

Instead, it's a language with no words that varies from person to person. Yet we all "speak" this language each minute of every day through our beliefs, feelings, and emotions. And our conversation is happening on both a conscious and subconscious level.

New discoveries linking the electromagnetic fields of the human heart (the place where our beliefs, feelings, and emotions are focused) to the magnetic field of the earth itself—the very field that connects all life—now give new meaning to the power of our conscious and subconscious beliefs.

Dr. Darren Weissman has devoted the bulk of his adult life to understanding the subconscious mind and the language of our beliefs—the codes that unlock our greatest potential. The LifeLine Technique Flow Chart that he developed, like DNA, is beautiful, elegant, and simple. It acts as a cosmic blueprint or road map for decoding the language of symptoms and stress. It bypasses the conscious thinking mind to lead us to our deepest and truest nature; we are all intelligently designed to heal, regenerate, and be whole.

Darren has already helped thousands of individuals awaken to their power, and he now invites you to go one step further. Building upon and bridging both ancient healing arts and philosophies and new breakthrough discoveries that integrate the mind, body, and spirit, he encourages us to recognize that we are part of the greatest shift of thinking in 5,000 years of recorded human history. We are recognizing that our personal choices have global implications.

In 2005, the magazine *Scientific American* published a special edition entitled "Crossroads for Planet Earth." In it, the contributors identified a number of scenarios that, if left unchecked, hold the potential to end civilization, and even life as we know it, on Earth. Through a number of essays and reports, experts in various fields present a strong case for a single, simple fact: our civilization cannot sustain the same path of violent competition, ever-expanding economies, depletion of resources, and growing contribution to climate change that we have traveled over the last 100 years. The point the experts make is that while each of the scenarios alone is catastrophic, *all* are happening right now.

And that's why your choices and this book are so important. Are we headed into an age of catastrophe, an age of peace, or possibly both? No one knows for certain. What we do know is that the physics linking heart-based focus and cooperation with what happens on Earth tells us that how we experience our changing world is largely up to us. The results of the discoveries are conclusive: what we feel has a direct effect upon what we experience. If we recognize our individual power of heart-based focus to create a world of peace and cooperation, and pool that power into a collective wave of influence, we may well discover that the hopeful future of our ancestors' visions is more than just a metaphor. We will have learned that we literally have within us the power to create a beautiful new world.

It all begins with us—with you. *Awakening to the Secret Code of Your Mind* is your user's guide to the personal changes that lead to that beautiful new world.

— **Gregg Braden**
Taos, New Mexico

✦✦✦ ✦✦✦

Introduction

" . . . we live in an interactive reality where we change the world around us by changing what happens inside of us while we're watching—that is, our thoughts, feelings, and beliefs. . . . From the healing of disease, to the length of our lives, to the success of our careers and relationships, everything that we experience as 'life' is directly linked to what we believe."

— Gregg Braden

You hold in your hands a complete system for changing your life if you choose to take action. This bold assertion is based on two premises: (1) fundamental and lasting change begins with understanding that you live, as Gregg Braden notes, in an "interactive reality" whose architect is the subconscious mind; and (2) to facilitate that change, you must make a *conscious* choice about how you will live your life—the choice between love and fear.

Faced with a barrage of daily messages about global peril, financial instability, ballooning unemployment, pandemic viruses, dwindling portfolios, disappearing life savings, and escalating wars, we might perceive this as a difficult choice to make. Many people feel that the world is teetering on the brink of destruction. There's a subconscious collective "thought virus" of helplessness, anxiety, and pessimism perpetuating the belief that there's little to no hope of averting a worldwide catastrophe. Feeling powerless and victimized, many people succumb to suffering.

Today, I'm offering you a different option—the power and the tools to choose love. I'm offering you a prism through which you can learn to see each and every experience, challenge, or stressful situation—whether it's a health, personal, or world crisis—as an opportunity to transform your life. I call this prism the *1-2-3 PLAN* (the Preliminary LifeLine Assessment Navigator) of *The LifeLine Technique.*

The LifeLine Technique is a philosophy of life; it's a science that connects you to consciousness, and a technology for quantum healing. It allows you to discover, interpret, and release the root causes of all physical pain and emotional symptoms, like stress and anxiety . . . emotions buried within the subconscious mind. In this book, you'll learn the three easy steps it takes to activate your subconscious mind, your body, and life's innate capacity for transformation and inner peace.

Arun Gandhi, the grandson of Mahatma Gandhi, says, "Peace starts with the self and then the whole world joins in."[1] World peace begins with inner peace. Based upon the work I've done with thousands of clients, I have concluded that the key to sustainable inner peace is discovering the running dialogue your body and life are having with you. The 1-2-3 PLAN of The LifeLine Technique will enable you to not only translate this language, but also to *create* your life through the power of your mind.

Creating the Life of Your Dreams

Sessions with The LifeLine Technique empower you to live an intentional, healthy, and passionate life. The secret to creating the life of your dreams is buried beneath the surface of your daily reality, within the subconscious mind. In his book *The Biology of Belief*, Bruce Lipton, Ph.D., explains:

> When it comes to sheer neurological processing abilities, the subconscious mind is millions of times more powerful than the conscious mind. If the desires of the conscious mind conflict with the programs of the subconscious mind, which "mind" do you think will win out? You can repeat the positive affirmation that you are lovable over and over or that your cancer tumor will shrink. But if, as a child, you heard over and over that you are worthless and sickly, those messages programmed in your subconscious mind will undermine your best conscious efforts to change your life.[2]

The conscious mind is perceived to be the driving force of life, but it actually only represents 2 to 10 percent of your awareness. The *sub*conscious mind makes up the other 90 to 98 percent. It directs the function of your 50 trillion–plus cells like a symphonic orchestra in perfect harmony. The subconscious mind is both a filter and a distiller of information, experiences, thoughts, and feelings—from your beating heart and the regeneration of your cells to food metabolism and waste elimination. The subconscious mind is also the storehouse of emotions, memories, and beliefs whose effects are vivid, hypnotic, illusionary, pervasive, and deep-seated. It's the reactive mind; it *reacts* to your environment so that you can adapt and survive. In other words, it shields and protects you like a tour guide through an uncharted land.

You can better understand the influence and power of the subconscious mind through this example: Imagine that your body is covered with a bright red itchy, painful rash. Notice how just reading about a rash causes you to scratch! How does having the "rash" make you feel? Angry? Frustrated? Or do you feel ashamed or insecure? If given a conscious choice, would you ever *choose* to have a bright red itchy, painful rash? Would you choose to feel angry, frustrated, ashamed, or insecure? Of course not—the rash and the emotions associated with it are reactive in nature!

You'd never consciously choose any unpleasant symptom, stressor, or disease; while at the same time you know that everyone experiences them—so where are they coming from? If symptoms don't stem from conscious choices, then they must be coming from the part of the mind and body that is reactive: the subconscious. This awareness is the first step to awakening to the secret code of your mind.

In my first book, *The Power of Infinite Love & Gratitude,* I shared a new paradigm for understanding symptoms, focusing on the subconscious mind. The only time you're aware of this part of you is when it's *speaking* to you through the *language* of symptoms. The rash is the vehicle that the subconscious mind uses to make you aware of the anger, frustration, shame, or insecurity that you didn't have the conscious tools, strategies, or support to process at an earlier time in your life. The LifeLine Technique takes any symptom or stress, and then through the power of your imagination and setting a positive intention about the experience, harmonizes and reprograms every cell in your body to mirror that intention. The end product is your power to consciously live and attract an intentional life.

While I'll discuss this concept in further detail later in these pages, the crucial point I want you to remember as you listen to your body or observe your life is that symptoms are gifts in strange wrapping paper—ones stemming from the subconscious mind. They represent the gap between your conscious awareness and subconscious knowing. When you have an experience that's painful, scary, or stressful and you lack the conscious resources to process it, the subconscious mind will initially create a gap as a means of protection to keep your spirit safe. In this book, you'll learn how to use the 1-2-3 PLAN of The LifeLine Technique to unwrap and appreciate these gifts. The universal healing frequency of Infinite Love & Gratitude is used to bridge the gap between the subconscious and conscious minds, activating the body to naturally work as it's designed . . . as a self-healing, regenerating, and whole organism.

The process of learning The LifeLine Technique is an evolutionary journey. My personal challenge in teaching or writing about this modality is that it's an original idea. There are things to compare it to, while at the same time there's nothing in the world quite like it. It truly is a secret code that, when discovered, awakens your heart to the beauty and passion of living. It's both scientific and spiritual, but in the end it's simply about love. As we all know, this emotion is the one thing that can't be defined; rather, it is an experience that's felt in your heart. Opening your mind and heart to the power of Infinite Love & Gratitude will forever change your life!

The Courage to Forgive

To create the greatest potential for lasting change, it's essential to bridge the gap between the subconscious and conscious minds. As Bruce Lipton noted, all of your experiences are intertwined in the matrix of the subconscious, resulting in what and how you currently think, feel, or believe. When the gap is bridged, you're able to make a conscious choice based on the moment, or what I refer to as *Present Time Consciousness* (PTC), instead of making a choice based on a subconscious reaction of fear or anger.

The following experience from Alice, a 49-year-young fiber artist who lives in South Carolina, demonstrates how a shift in perspective and a conscious choice can change your destiny:

> In early 2007, I began experiencing heavy vaginal bleeding, as well as frequent and urgent urination. During the first 24 hours of the onset of my menstrual cycle, I had to stay in bed. In mid-October, I finally went to the doctor. She said that more than likely I had fibroid tumors, and she ordered a MRI, which confirmed the diagnosis: there were several fibroids the size of small tangerines. While reviewing the pictures with me, the doctor also noted that I had two spleens, which she said was highly unusual. When I asked her what I should do about the fibroids, she recommended that I get a hysterectomy.

I didn't want to have an operation, and sincerely believed that there was another way to help my body heal itself. Dr. Darren Weissman immediately came to mind. I had recently attended his lecture at the "I Can Do It!" conference in Tampa. His kindness, enthusiasm, and radiating love and the explanation of his technique made me an instant believer in possibilities I previously hadn't considered. I immediately purchased and read his book *The Power of Infinite Love & Gratitude.*

In November, a friend gave me a gift—a session with Dr. Darren at his clinic in the Chicago area. I flew in the Tuesday before Thanksgiving; my appointment was the next morning. Dr. Darren spent more than an hour with me, both talking, and conducting a LifeLine Technique session.

What struck me most during the session was his saying that the imbalance in my reproductive organs was the result of subconscious anger and the lack of forgiveness associated with early-childhood sexual abuse. I confirmed that this was true— a relative had repeatedly sexually abused me, beginning at the age of three. Although I no longer was in contact with this relative, I still had a great deal of anger, which I knew had impacted intimate relationships with men throughout my life.

This healing method is *not* for sissies! You have to be willing and able to examine the dark parts of yourself and expose them to the light of love in order to let them go. I left Dr. Darren's office with hugs, lots of nutritional supplements, and tons to process. Most important, I left there with a feeling of hopefulness for healing.

I spent Thanksgiving with my children and friends. It was a day full of love and fun. That night, I read Dr. Darren's book again. I meditated, using all the forgiveness methods I knew to release the pain and anger I had been harboring. I remember going to bed thanking God, the goddesses, the Universe, and the ancestors for my life and everything in it. For the first time, I also said a prayer of forgiveness for the relative who had abused me.

Since I'm not a "mall shopper," I planned to spend the day after Thanksgiving resting, grateful for time alone. About noon on that Friday, I went to the restroom and felt three or four "lumps" fall out of my vagina and into the toilet. There was minimal pain and, upon examination, very little blood. My first thought was to retrieve these "lumps" from the toilet and put them in the freezer. However, I have a roommate and knew she would be uncomfortable if she discovered them there! So I flushed them.

I called the gynecologist's office for an appointment first thing Monday morning, and the doctor fit me right in. I explained to her in graphic detail what had transpired on Friday at noon. Her exact response was: "Nonsense!" I insisted that she send me for another MRI, which was arranged for that afternoon. On Tuesday morning, I was back in her office for the results. We looked at the MRI together. The fibroids were gone! The doctor insisted that the radiologist had sent someone else's MRI instead of mine.

"Wouldn't my double spleen show up on this MRI?" I asked the doctor.

"Yes, of course," she replied.

We looked at the MRI together. The double spleen was there, but there were no fibroid tumors! My body had healed itself!

That was two years ago, and the fibroids have *not* recurred. Since then, I have referred many of my friends to Dr. Darren, and they have all experienced amazing healing results. I believe in Infinite Love & Gratitude! As a matter of fact, I think this method should be called Infinite, Unconditional Love & Gratitude!

Thank you, Dr. Darren. You are a channel and a facilitator of healing. I love you.[3]

Illness, disease, pain, and stress are symptoms. And symptoms, as I said earlier, are gifts from the subconscious mind. More important, they are *necessary* to awaken you to the power of transformation. Experience is the only way to truly understand how the power of your mind is able to unleash the pure potential you *already* possess for healing, wholeness, and peace.

Choose Inner Peace Today

Let's set an intention together: *Today I'm choosing to feel inner peace.* I'd like you to take a moment to visualize your life in this state. Based upon your heart's desire and the destiny of your soul, imagine that you're already your most powerful and peaceful self. This may be challenging; however, you can do it!

What does your life look like? What are you doing that you're not doing now? How does it *feel* to connect to your life in this way? Set your intention as if you're already there using the statement "I am ____." For example, "I am confident and loving." Take some time right now and imagine yourself living your intention. Notice how it feels to imagine being "confident and loving." This feeling is your LifeLine to Source.

Write down three points on a separate piece of paper or in a journal. This list will be used as the basis for transforming the symptoms and stress of your body and life into intentions of infinite possibilities.

⊕ ⊕ ⊕

Awakening to the Secret Code of Your Mind is not just another "how-to" book; it's a self-empowerment book. You'll not only learn *how,* but you'll also understand *why* your body, your life, and the world are expressing such symptoms as chaos, chronic pain, anxiety, or financial challenges. This book contains the tools necessary to transform your life and the step-by-step action plan for being your best self.

Anyone and everyone can learn The LifeLine Technique. The process requires study, commitment, and passion and can be extended to the level of mastery through a certification process of weekend seminars that I teach. Some may understand it right away—something in your heart will be activated . . . a familiar feeling of wholeness, comfort, and confidence. Others may think I'm speaking a foreign language. Either way, looking at symptoms and stress as a form of communication *is* a new language—a dialogue that stems from the subconscious mind—and the 1-2-3 PLAN of The LifeLine Technique is your simple decoder.

Expanding the Frontiers of Consciousness

Life as you've previously known it is about to change as you begin to understand the intimate, collective connection we all share, which manifests as symptoms and stressors of daily life. The process of bridging the gap between the conscious and subconscious minds in and of itself will expand your perception of possibilities and awaken you to your potential for inner peace. That's why I've written this book: to provide a comprehensive understanding of the mind and a way to access its power in any given moment.

There are two sections of this book:

— In **Part I: Breaking the Code of Your Mind,** Chapters 1 through 8 reveal the science of the heart, the power of choice, and the role perception plays in health and happiness. You'll read life-affirming testimonials about The LifeLine Technique that will cause you to question your current view while at the same time will prepare your soul to access your highest potential, regardless of circumstances.

— Along with pictures and diagrams, Chapters 9 through 29, which compose **Part II: Interpreting the Code of Your Mind,** reinforce the science and philosophy that are the cornerstones of each of the 16 steps of The LifeLine Technique Flow Chart—the blueprint of the subconscious mind. In this section, I share the simplicity of the 1-2-3 PLAN and its power to attract the life of your dreams. Be prepared to cry, laugh, and be inspired by the amazing paradigm shifts resulting from the power of Infinite Love & Gratitude!

In these pages, you will learn the sacred art of shape-shifting the illusionary nature of symptoms and stress into opportunities for healing and thriving. The 1-2-3 PLAN is the first step for transforming a reactive life into one of purpose.*

The Way of Change

Emotion is the energy that moves you. When you find your life stuck in a pattern—repeatedly reacting to the same person, allergen, food, or time of day . . . or any other life experience . . . in a negative or painful way—it's a sign that the energy moving you is motivated by survival and protection rather than your present circumstances. The LifeLine Law of Transformation and Creation states: *Emotions transform energy; energy creates movement; movement is change; and change is the essence of life.* More than the fear of death, it's the fear of *change* that keeps people stuck in a cycle of self-destruction and self-defeat. When you're able to embrace change, follow your heart, and go with the flow, you're emotionally flowing through life, and life is emotionally flowing through you.

Awakening to The LifeLine Technique has forever changed my life, and it's with a humble heart that I now share the sacred wisdom that holds the promise for you to discover inner peace. Seventeenth-century scientist and philosopher Blaise Pascal once wrote: "We know the truth, not only by the reason, but also by the heart." The truth is simple . . . open your heart. Choosing love is the only solution.

My intention in writing this book is to inspire you regardless of who you are, where you are in life, or what you've been through. As a teacher, I have a passion for igniting the hearts of whoever resonates with the knowing that there must be another way. You must answer your own calling and be willing to embrace the truth.

---

*The LifeLine Technique is a complete system and requires hands-on training to master. If your goal is mastery, check out the Information and Resources section in the back of the book to learn about becoming a Certified LifeLine Practitioner.

Are you ready to acknowledge how powerful you really are? You're *already* pure love, beautiful, special, accepting, forgiving, grateful, compassionate, kind, intelligent, successful, funny, creative, joyous, wonderful, fantastic, passionate, humble, confident, and peaceful beyond measure. This is *your* truth. You'll now realize with your "real eyes" that when you're feeling anything but powerful, beautiful, and special, it's your subconscious mind *urging* you to grab The LifeLine . . . urging you to choose love.

Choose love. Choose to be an ambassador of light in a world that so sorely needs a way out of the darkness of pain, shame, guilt, and fear. The simple act of awakening to the power of the mind holds the promise of hope for a parent whose child tragically dies, for people who feel victimized by their bodies, or for the survivors of a town ravaged by a natural disaster. *Awakening to the Secret Code of Your Mind* enables you to unleash your natural capacity to heal and thrive.

Would you read this book if you knew, with absolute certainty, that it was a call to action, a road map for humanity, the passageway for creating powerful shifts in consciousness to awaken and embrace yourself with love? Guess what . . . it is!

With Infinite Love & Gratitude,
Dr. Darren R. Weissman

⊕⊕⊕ ⊕⊕⊕

PART I

Breaking the Code
of Your Mind

*"There is something in nature that forms patterns.
We, as part of nature, also form patterns. The mind is
like the wind and the body is like the sand; if you want
to know how the wind is blowing, you can look at the sand."*

— Bonnie Bainbridge Cohen

CHAPTER 1

Love's Universal Healing Power

"What science can't explain, it doesn't see. This
includes beauty, devotion, faith, inspiration, nobility,
compassion, empathy, fate, intuition, and love itself.
Are we really claiming these are fictions or illusions?"

— Deepak Chopra, M.D.

Although the concept that "love heals" is as ancient as the human race, it was not something I always understood. I studied chiropractic, acupuncture, homeopathy, naturopathy, magnetotherapy, shamanism, natural healing, Neuro-Linguistic Programming, Applied Kinesiology, Total Body Modification, Neuro Emotional Technique, and Chinese energetic medicine, searching for *the* answer to the eternal question that Caroline Myss posed in her bellwether book *Why People Don't Heal and How They Can.* Like all major transformations, in order for the answer to emerge from within, I needed external catalysts.

I was introduced to the "I love you" hand gesture in 1998 by my cousin Rob Morgan, who worked as an intern in my office in preparation for becoming the first deaf chiropractor to graduate from the Palmer College of Chiropractic. After a full day of observing my work with clients, Rob held up his hand to me in the "I love you" sign.

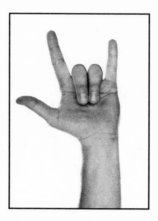

I felt a warm, powerful, and peaceful feeling as he did so. Intrigued by my internal reaction, using muscle testing, I checked Rob for weak reflex points on his body. When I found one, I held my hand next to his body in the "I love you" sign mode. The reflex instantly "locked out," as Rob and I looked at each other in amazement. I didn't realize then the impact of that moment.

Three years later, I received an e-mail from my friend Greg. It contained photographs of Dr. Masaru Emoto's groundbreaking water-crystal research. Emoto, a doctor of alternative medicine and a visionary researcher, had made an amazing discovery that was opening the world's eyes to new vistas of health and healing. I later found information about his work in his book *Messages from Water:*

> Human vibrational energy—thoughts, words, ideas, and music—affects the molecular structure of water. It is the very same water that comprises over 70 percent of a mature human body and covers the same amount of our planet. . . . The quality of our life is directly connected to the quality of our water.[1]

Dr. Emoto exposed test tubes filled with tap water to words, music, and positive thoughts and then froze them. He extracted a frozen crystal from each tube, and using a process called dark-field microscopy, he examined and photographed them all. Each formation was different, documenting the essence of water's power—its consciousness—and the instantaneous impact thoughts, words, and actions have on its molecular structure.[2]

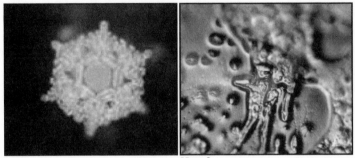

Love.   Hate.[3]

Dr. Emoto's work provided tangible empirical evidence of what many conscious visionaries—from Louise L. Hay; Debbie Shapiro; and Candace Pert, Ph.D.; to Bruce Lipton, Ph.D.; David Hawkins, M.D., Ph.D.; and Gregg Braden—had already been espousing and teaching for many years before: emotions impact the health of the body, as well as our sense of well-being. Dr. Emoto's work just showed us *how.*

The final catalyst to my awakening was triggered by my friend and colleague Dr. Ingrid Maes, who challenged me to look past the fear blocking my path and see, with clarity of vision, my soul's destiny. In February 2002, I channeled The LifeLine Technique Flow Chart (see page 78), a logarithmic blueprint of the subconscious mind. The vision appeared, as ornate and detailed as a Tibetan sand mandala. I was concerned that if I moved, the vision of the Flow Chart would dissipate into thin air. I scribbled words and drew lines, arrows, and geometric shapes on a piece of scrap paper handed to me by my fiancée (and now wife), Sarit. I saw everything I'd ever studied, as well as images perceived for the very first time. They were woven together in a seamless, matrix-like framework.

I knew intuitively that this was the unified system of healing and wholeness I had been seeking, and because of Dr. Emoto's water-crystal research, I knew love and gratitude were essential components of deciphering this secret code of the mind. Thus began my understanding of the potential power of Infinite Love & Gratitude and the collapse of the illusory walls of fear that had been holding me back from knowing *my* truth.

I now know unequivocally that Infinite Love & Gratitude is a universal healing frequency. Coupled with The LifeLine Technique Flow Chart to decipher the pain, fear, or stress in your body and life, it is the foundation for your mind's journey to inner peace. With this book, you'll learn how and why so that you can bridge the gaps in your life that are inhibiting you from experiencing and creating peace in your heart and freedom in your life.

Teaching People to Heal Themselves

From the outset, it was clear that teaching people about the power of Infinite Love & Gratitude and how to use The LifeLine Technique had the potential to transform the world of health and healing on a global scale. This vision soon became my mission. In the beginning, only a few people believed it and worked tirelessly with me to manifest it. We were, to borrow the famous phrase of renowned anthropologist Margaret Mead, "a small group of thoughtful, committed citizens" who passionately shared the power of Infinite Love & Gratitude as a universal healing frequency with whoever wanted to learn.

For close to ten years, I've helped thousands of people *transform themselves* from imbalances in their bodies that their allopathic (Western-medical) doctors labeled "incurable." Even more, I've been fortunate enough to teach people around the world how to activate the power of their minds to transform their own lives and use it to help others.

As noted in the Introduction, The LifeLine Technique can be learned by anyone and everyone. The following two stories demonstrate that you can experience the benefits even with just the initial training.

Dolly lived with cats all her life, but in 2004 her body began to "speak" to her with an allergy to them. That all changed when she learned The LifeLine Technique:

> One day while I was waiting for a bus, I decided to go through The LifeLine Technique Flow Chart for myself, giving myself Infinite Love & Gratitude as I did so. When I got home that evening, I immediately noticed that I wasn't having allergic symptoms around my cats or with any other cats. I didn't even have the intention of "treating" the cat allergy with The LifeLine Technique. I just conducted the session for practice and was amazed by what happened![4]

In another case, Mary shared the following experience she had within a few weeks of attending her first LifeLine Technique training:

> I have a friend who has a ten-year-old daughter named Lisa. For several years, Lisa's body had been expressing the symptom of psoriasis on her torso, arms, legs, face, and scalp. Her family physician prescribed many topical ointments, but they did nothing to alleviate the symptoms. After the first training, I contacted my friend to see whether I might be of some help to Lisa. I was thrilled when they both said yes!
>
> Being totally inexperienced with The LifeLine Technique, I referred to my training notes throughout our sessions. I used the 1-2-3 PLAN at each session. Lisa had a hard time creating an intention (Step 2), so I used Louise Hay's book *You Can Heal Your Life* to find affirmations that would help her to do so. The affirmations were "I love and approve of myself" and "I deserve the best, and I accept it now." The subconscious emotions that came up during the sessions included anger at self, lack of self-worth, and withheld feelings. Each time an emotion came up, I harmonized it with Infinite Love & Gratitude.

When Lisa came in for the fifth session, I noticed that she only had little white "dots" on her arms where the psoriasis had been. I also noticed that her scalp and face were totally clear. By the sixth session, all signs of the psoriasis were gone. I told Lisa how great her skin looked, and she beamed the most beautiful smile!

I am amazed by the power of The LifeLine Technique and so grateful to have it in my life![5]

You Are a Barometer for All of Humanity

In Gregg Braden's book *Secrets of the Lost Mode of Prayer,* he shares the results of a study conducted by the International Peace Project in the Middle East, which was first published in *The Journal of Conflict Resolution* in December of 1988:

> During the Israeli-Lebanese war of the early 1980s, researchers trained a group of people to "feel" peace in their bodies rather than simply think about peace in their minds or pray for peace to occur.
>
> On specific days of the month, at specific times each day, these people were positioned throughout the war-torn areas of the Middle East. During the window of time that they were feeling peace, terrorist activities stopped, crimes against people lessened, emergency-room visits declined, and traffic accidents dropped off in number. When the people stopped expressing these feelings, the statistics reversed. These studies confirmed the earlier results: When a small percentage of the population achieved peace within themselves, that peace was reflected in the world around them.[6]

The current state of your life—as well as your physical, emotional, and spiritual well-being—is a barometer for all of humanity and Mother Earth. With the power of Infinite Love & Gratitude and the decoder of your mind—The LifeLine Technique—you'll be able to expand your capacity to thrive and live a passionate and purposeful life, which is the ultimate expression of peace. Because we're all one, no matter what your race, nationality, gender, religion, political views, beliefs, or social status, when your life resonates with inner peace, it becomes the harbinger for the world you're helping to create. Every shared experience reaffirms to me the innate capacity of the body to heal itself when it's given the proper conditions: Infinite Love & Gratitude for any and every experience!

Recognizing the growing trend toward alternative approaches to health and medicine, some scientists are attempting to document the healing power of love, opening the way for understanding *how* you transform your reality when you make a choice to live your life based upon it, regardless of how fearful you may feel. One thing you can be sure of: unconditional self-love is the place to begin.

⊕⊕⊕ ⊕⊕⊕

CHAPTER 2

The Science of Love

"When we experience the unconditional nature of love,
we open to a vista of unlimited healing power."
— Debbie Shapiro

In 1991, the Institute of HeartMath (IHM) Research Center was established for the purpose of exploring how the heart communicates with the brain, and the impact of that communication on the physiological function of the body. Since its inception, IHM has become a highly regarded, global leader in psychophysiology, stress management, and the physiology of heart-brain research. Among the goals of one of IHM's initial research projects was to determine the physiological ramifications of love and other positive emotions. The findings are fascinating, and they include the following ideas:

- Feeling love and sincere appreciation increases the coherence of the heart's energy-wave pattern, altering the electromagnetic field emanating from this area.[1]

- Positive emotions (such as love) increase harmony and coherence in the heart's rhythms and improve the balance in the nervous system.[2]

- Negative emotions lead to increased disorder in the heart's rhythms, as well as disordered rhythms in the autonomic nervous system, thereby adversely affecting the rest of the body.[3]

Additionally, researchers discovered that the heart's energy field is about 60 times more powerful than that of the brain; it can be measured several feet away from the body.[4] This means that the energy field of the heart is always touching, and interacting and commingling with, the hearts of other people, sometimes acting as a gauge of subtle electromagnetic communication between people.[5] In other words, IHM has found a way to measure and validate those "vibes" we feel when we first meet or interact with others!

While IHM's work is just a tiny fraction of the ongoing research seeking to document the function of the heart, what we now have is a scientific basis for understanding *how* that function impacts mental clarity, creativity, emotional balance, physical well-being, and personal effectiveness.[6]

Everything emanates from the heart—love, passion, music, beauty, compassion, empathy, and faith. In fact, as Louise L. Hay has been teaching all of us for the past quarter century, "Love is the miracle cure. Loving ourselves works miracles in our lives."[7]

Documenting The LifeLine Technique

When I first awakened to The LifeLine Technique, I felt it was important to provide some empirical evidence for the transformational experiences I'd been witnessing. Inspired by the research of Masaru Emoto, and with the assistance of my friend and colleague Dr. Tom Bayne, we used dark-field microscopy to conduct live blood-cell analyses before and after a LifeLine Technique session. Because blood is nearly 90 percent water, I hypothesized that, like Dr. Emoto's work with crystals, we should witness a change in it.

We collected and documented scores of blood slides taken immediately before and immediately after sessions with The LifeLine Technique. Many of the pictures, like the two examples reprinted here, were first published in *The Power of Infinite Love & Gratitude.*

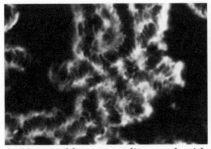 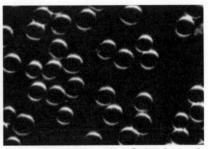

A 41-year-old woman diagnosed with breast cancer.

Using the power of Infinite Love & Gratitude, released subconscious feelings of depression associated with being emotionally and verbally abused by her husband.

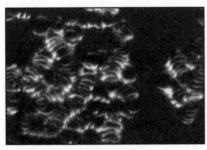 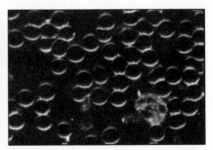

A 53-year-old woman with symptoms of insomnia.

Using the power of Infinite Love & Gratitude, released subconscious fears about her future due to the reorganization of the company where she worked.

Recently, I received an e-mail from a registered nurse and nutritionist who had a session with a Certified LifeLine Practitioner. She conducted her own experiments using a dark-field microscope:

> I just wanted to send you a quick note and tell you about the difference in the dark-field microscope pictures of my pre- and post-sessions with The LifeLine Technique. The pre-session picture was very toxic. Not only was it hard to get the drop of blood to form after the finger prick, but the red blood cells were all stuck together (aggregation); and there were a fair number of bacterial spheres, target cells, and large crystals. After the session, the finger stick formed a quick bead, and the red blood cells were floating side by side. I saw fewer bacteria and no target cells. The large crystals were reduced to tiny broken-glass-like clusters. I have never seen anything like this before![8]

Understanding Through Experience

Because The LifeLine Technique is best understood through experience, I feel it's important to share with you the testimonials I have received from people whose lives have profoundly changed as a result of sessions with this revolutionary healing modality. Not only do these experiences include people with whom I've personally done sessions, but they're also from those who have had sessions with other Certified LifeLine Practitioners (CLPs). Every CLP has a personal experience with The LifeLine Technique. They came to the first training program from all walks of life—laypeople with no background in health or healing, stay-at-home moms, senior citizens, healing-arts practitioners, bodyworkers, allopathic nurses and doctors, psychotherapists, social workers, and life coaches—and then decided to become certified.

Hope was an IT specialist when she first learned about The LifeLine Technique in 2007. Today, she is a Certified LifeLine Practitioner based in the southern U.S. Her determination to persevere and to trust her inner knowing that there was another way has inspired and touched the hearts of the thousands of people who read her postings on the electronic bulletin board set up for those who have participated in The LifeLine Technique training. Hope's path to healing is still unfolding. However, she has given me permission to share her story with you:

> My LifeLine journey began on my 50th birthday. My parents wanted to send me on a trip somewhere, and I opted for the Hay House "I Can Do It!" conference in Tampa. After consulting with a friend who is also a medical intuitive, I decided to change some of my conference workshop selections. Unfortunately, I wasn't familiar with any of the other authors and thus wasn't sure which to choose. Then I saw the listing for Dr. Darren Weissman. I said to myself, *Hmm . . . Infinite Love & Gratitude. That sounds like something I could use!*
>
> I was in the third row, and for some reason, as Darren started to talk, I began to cry. This continued for most of the two-hour presentation. I remember after he had finished, there was an elderly gentleman who walked up to the stage and said, "Excuse me, sir." Speaking to Darren and the audience, he explained that he had been unable to bend or separate the fingers of his right hand due to an odd side effect of some epidural anesthesia for a procedure six weeks prior. He then made the hand sign for Infinite Love & Gratitude.
>
> I cried again as I realized that I wasn't the only one who had been profoundly affected by what had occurred in that room. To this day I cannot explain what happened to me that afternoon. The one thing I was absolutely clear about was that The LifeLine Technique was something I was supposed to be doing for the rest of my life. I signed up for the first level of the training, which was to be held in Chicago two months later.
>
> The Conscious Body–Conscious Mind training was incredibly powerful. When I returned home, I practiced on friends and others daily. I was amazed that I was able to successfully help facilitate the transformation of a woman who had been diagnosed with autoimmune anemia to avoid a splenectomy. She was the mother

of a friend, and I had never met her. All of these sessions were conducted over the telephone since she lived in another state.

I had a number of physical and emotional issues as well— from diabetes and thyroid and pituitary insufficiency to diagnoses of major depressive disorder, panic disorder, and post-traumatic stress disorder. Consequently, I had been taking antidepressant medications since my early 20s. I was diagnosed with what the doctor termed "treatment-resistant depression," and the more recent SSRIs (selective serotonin reuptake inhibitors) I took had to be changed at least twice a year, as their efficacy quickly faded. I had to slowly titrate down on one and up on a new one to avoid early worsening, so there was always a four-week period of sheer misery during this switch where I essentially had nothing in my system to help. My former co-workers learned to ignore me when I sat and cried nonstop at my desk or had the occasional burst of rage.

With all my experiences and my constant need to understand things, I ended up knowing more about antidepressants than many family doctors. Over the years, I attempted to get off the medication and became suicidal, requiring hospitalization. I finally came to the sad acceptance that I would have to take antidepressants for the rest of my life.

It seemed that no matter what I was working on for myself with The LifeLine Technique, be it physical or emotional, there was a constant return to the internalized or disconnected emotions associated with trauma at the ages of 4 and 11. I could feel the deep sadness, defeat, and isolation of myself at four; and it astounded me, as I always think of children as being pure joy. I never thought a child could feel that way. I was surprised to see these same events and emotions show up when I did a session to download the vision board I had created during the LifeLine training. It was proof to me that no matter how much emotional work I had done in the past, these traumas and their emotional remnants had permeated my entire life, affecting every future experience I would have. I knew as well that these events were the subconscious source of the depression.

With the assistance of my medical doctor, I weaned myself off the antidepressants. I felt so much better. However, I found there were some residual challenges masked by the pharmaceuticals—some anger and impatience. I consistently gave myself LifeLine sessions for a few weeks, and although there was progress, it seemed to be slow and resistant.

I see an alternative-health doctor/nutritionist, and I was quite irritable while in his office one day. The doctor explained that it can take up to 12 months for the body to fully clear the effects that antidepressants have on its serotonin receptors, making it hard for it to use the serotonin it naturally creates. A lightbulb went off in my head. I decided to give myself a LifeLine session with the intention to have clean, completely open, and receptive serotonin receptors. I also included insulin receptors in my intention to help with the type 2 diabetes.

I was quite astounded by the results of the sessions! What came up were repeated messages about my inability to be receptive, which is so true for me. I am always the "giver" and have had trouble receiving compliments, gifts, or even friendship. The metaphors between life and the body are amazing.

Within a few sessions, both the insulin receptors and the serotonin receptors showed up as being clear. I have been off insulin for more than six months and completely off antidepressants for more than nine months. The last session I conducted focusing on the serotonin receptors had one emotion: fear of change. I was amazed that the occasional irritability and short temper completely subsided since the work on the receptors, and I am a different person!

I've been through some really difficult circumstances of late and have had devastating financial and other news. I have to admit I had some doubts about whether or not I would fall back into depression, but I haven't! Loving myself unconditionally and staying in Present Time Consciousness (PTC)—being authentic, especially about my feelings, and feeling them as they occur—has kept me moving forward.

What a triumph this is for me! I have had years of therapy and used every healing modality to free myself of this pain. I've always said that if I was ever able to get off the medication, it would be a true miracle. That miracle is now a reality. It's truly a catharsis in my life. If I never see another client, the cost of learning The LifeLine Technique was fully worth it just for this victory. I am absolutely blessed to have stumbled into Darren's seminar "by accident," only to have the rest of my life fall blissfully into place. He is truly a visionary, and I am honored to have been trained by him in this incredible life-changing technique.[9]

Like a tree budding in the spring, The LifeLine Technique session heralds the beginning of a new season in your life— one that's filled with joy and peace. As we learned from Hope, commitment, persistence, and conviction are integral when you're on a mission to heal and transform your life. By choosing to love herself unconditionally and refusing to stay "stuck" in her circumstances, Hope has demonstrated experiential evidence and tangible proof of the science of love.

⊕⊕⊕ ⊕⊕⊕

CHAPTER 3

What Do You Choose?

"A great revolution in just one single individual will
help achieve a change in the destiny of a society and,
further, will enable a change in the destiny of humankind."
— Daisaku Ikeda

In 2008, I had the opportunity to be one of the featured speakers, along with Dr. Michael Bernard Beckwith, on the Ocean of Gratitude Cruise, produced by Karol Avalon.[1] More than 200 people cruised to Cozumel, Mexico; Costa Rica; and Panama with the goal of exploring new paradigms for living with gratitude and achieving the lives of their dreams. While on the cruise, I met a multitalented songwriter and visual artist by the name of Shawn Gallaway. This modern-day troubadour's repertoire includes a song whose lyrics embody The LifeLine Technique philosophy:

I can see laughter
or I can see tears
I see a choice
Love or fear
What do you choose?[2]

Why is it important to choose love over fear? Dr. Emoto's photographs demonstrate the transformation of water crystals when they're exposed to the words *I hate you*. One of the most virulent forms of fear, hate creates dense, mudlike structures that look similar to cancer cells; while the words *Love* and *Gratitude* cause the formation of a unique, delicate, and beautiful crystal. Which of those two crystals do you think will most effectively conduct the living system of energy[3] that makes up your body? And how do you think fear impacts your body's function?

Choosing Love

In March 2009, accompanied by a team of Certified LifeLine Practitioners, I taught The LifeLine Technique in Australia for the first time. The experience profoundly transformed my life and deepened my understanding of the power of Infinite Love & Gratitude. I recently received an e-mail from a woman named Genevieve, one of the participants in the training, who lives in Perth, Australia. Genevieve's courageous experience exemplifies how our thoughts, beliefs, and actions can transform reality when we choose love:

> Recently, something happened that perhaps typifies the amazing difference the power of Infinite Love & Gratitude has made in my life. A stranger attempted to break into our house while my husband and I were there—in other words, a home invasion. I called the police. We thought there were two intruders, so my husband was in the back of the house and I was in the front. The man became more and more aggressive; he attempted to pull off the security door to get in our front door. I realized he might break in before the police arrived. I had the thought: *I need to protect myself,* followed by another thought to get a knife from the kitchen. But before I had sufficient time to move a muscle, yet another thought came: *I choose love.* I simply stood there with my hands in the Infinite Love & Gratitude sign, and started

saying aloud, "Infinite Love & Gratitude." My husband joined me, and we both stood there giving it our all!

This angry, aggressive man quickly became calmer and calmer. By the time the police arrived, about five minutes later, he was *lying down on our front lawn* with a knife by his side! He'd certainly had different intentions at the beginning. But that all changed with the power of Infinite Love & Gratitude!

He said to the police, "I know this doesn't look good, but I'm not a bad person." As he was being taken away, I overheard him say, "Please don't put me in there!" as he was being placed in the back of the police vehicle. His voice was that of a very young child; the tone spoke volumes about his childhood.

Infinite Love & Gratitude has opened my heart in ways I didn't know possible. The course in South Australia—coupled with Shawn Gallaway's song "I Choose Love," which I've been listening to almost daily—gifted me with the ability to literally choose love at a time when I could have easily chosen a weapon. Home invasion is a fear I overcame with love. . . . Your technique is a profound gift to the world![4]

The Survival System

When we experience fear, the subconscious system of survival is in charge. The *acute human stress response,* as defined by a group of medical doctors, psychotherapists, and biomedical researchers in the October 2004 issue of the journal *Psychosomatics,* is either "freeze, flight, fight, or fright."[5] This survival mechanism is an efficient system that hijacks both your biology and behavior, allowing you to take action during traumatic experiences when the conscious mind freezes or withdraws in terror.

Think of the experiences you've heard about where someone single-handedly lifted a car off of a person being crushed. Superman? No! The power of the subconscious mind. On the flip side, imagine being on a hike and suddenly seeing a mountain lion. The most likely subconscious survival response would be to run, right? During that heightened state of terror, you would probably break Olympic records! But even when you finally get to a safe location, the memory of the mountain lion continues to haunt you. Over time, the fear lingers; it morphs into worry, insecurity, phobia, and anxiety. Maybe it also morphs into an addiction because you had a shot of tequila when you got to a safe location. Now, drinking tequila seems to activate a subtle but powerful feeling of safety.

That moment of terror is locked in your subconscious mind. Fast-forward ten years—as far as you can tell, you're happy and carefree, and you only drink tequila on "special occasions" that you can't quite identify. You may even resume hiking, although you only go when there are large groups, and you always carry a large stick. Just because you're not *aware* of the fear doesn't mean it's no longer there. The subconscious mind protects the spirit. Every time there's a situation in your life that your *subconscious* perceives as dangerous, scary, or challenging, it's as if you're confronting that mountain lion all over again. You may not literally run away, but *subconsciously* the wall is put up. In that moment of fear your subconscious mind perceives, the eyes through which you're looking at the world are the ones that first saw that mountain lion. (You can substitute other experiences—for example, a broken heart, shock, injuries, assault, accidents, or even abandonment—for the mountain lion!)

Meanwhile, as described earlier, the subconscious mind is also in charge of every automatic and autonomic aspect of your body's function, including digestion, blood flow, immunity, and organ function. The survival mode is like an ambulance siren . . . all the cars on the road pull over to the side until the emergency vehicle has passed. When you subconsciously experience fear, your body immediately shifts to survival mode, and just like those cars on the side of the road, its functions don't "move" until it perceives that the emergency has passed.

Igniting Love

The LifeLine Technique is a quantum technology—that is, it works at the level of the body's energetic field—to deactivate the survival patterns of fear. I would like to share the story of Julia, 13, who had been experiencing chronic and relentless stomachaches, which began at the age of 6. The following is an excerpt from a letter to me from Julia's mother:

> Among the many, many things we used were: antacids, Pepto-Bismol, herbal tea, meditation, massage, visualization techniques, sleeping with a wedge pillow, and numerous changes in her diet. So many nights I would find Julia on the Internet looking for home cures for stomachaches in her desperate search for relief. Nothing worked. Finally, I took her to a pediatric gastrointestinal specialist. The doctor prescribed acid blockers for six weeks. This seemed to help a little, but caused secondary stomach pains. When we went back, the doctor said, "Just keep her on the acid blockers for a few more months." This seemed like crazy advice, and at about the same time, I first learned of your practice. I took Julia off the acid blockers and made an appointment with you.
>
> Without knowing our family history, you correctly discovered that Julia had subconscious issues from a time during which she felt very unsafe—a time when all the adults around her were also worried and unable to reassure her—when she was five or six years old. What you didn't know is that Julia's little sister was diagnosed with kidney cancer at that time. You were able to identify Julia's deep-seated fears and set her free.
>
> Julia had a total of four visits with you, and two more to learn the Emotional Freedom Technique from another practitioner in your clinic. *She has not had a stomachache since that very first visit with you six months ago!* To say this is miraculous is an understatement.[6]

How do you know when you're stuck in a pattern of fear? Everyone's journey is different, and as a result, the symptoms that manifest have a different and unique story. If you're not living a passionate and joy-filled life; if you don't *consciously* choose love in the face of a stressful or terrifying situation; if your body is chronically speaking to you with symptoms that don't go away, no matter what, then there's a subconscious pattern ready to be decoded so that your light can shine.

All symptoms are the signal the subconscious mind uses when you're at war with yourself and MIA (missing in action) in your own life. They are the flares seeking to guide you back to the present time, the time to choose love, and the time to know inner peace. Remember, symptoms are gifts in strange wrapping paper. When these gifts are uncovered, you're opening your heart and mind to learning what it truly means to be whole.

⊕⊕⊕ ⊕⊕⊕

CHAPTER 4

The Measure of Healing

*"Of one thing I am certain, the body is not the
measure of healing—peace is the measure."*

— attributed to George Melton

Kelly, 42, first came to see me at the suggestion of a friend.
She had one child and wanted to become pregnant again. She
had recently experienced a stillbirth during the 31st week of
pregnancy.

Kelly longed to have a second child; while at the same time,
she was filled with intense grief, guilt, and fear—fear that she
wouldn't become pregnant again. She also had an overwhelming
fear of another stillbirth. Three months after this traumatic event,
she began receiving sessions with The LifeLine Technique. Kelly
was able to move through the grief and suffering, and she became
pregnant by the fourth session. This is the letter she sent me a year
after the birth of her daughter, Faith, on the anniversary of the
stillbirth of the son she lovingly named Montana Skye:

> Today is Montana Skye's birthday—what a gift. As I think
> about him, I can't help but reflect on all those who supported me

through my loss and helped me connect back to Infinite Love & Gratitude! You're one of many, but an extra-special one indeed.

I will never forget my amazement upon experiencing The LifeLine Technique for the first time and physically feeling the grief move through my body. Nor will I forget the ways in which you supported me in my intention to have another baby, even when I doubted my own core beliefs. Faith was all giggles today; I swear Montana is around her and all of us today."[1]

The Truth of Healing

Many people equate the word *healing* with being asymptomatic or experiencing a dramatic change. They judge their progress based on the absence of symptoms. Most people do experience total relief or a dramatic reduction of symptoms after a single session with The LifeLine Technique. However, unless people realize that the sign of illness—whether it's physical or emotional—is an *opportunity* for their bodies and lives to be transformed at the deepest of levels, they will not *heal*. Symptoms are gifts that, when "unwrapped," lead to the most extraordinary truths of our lives.[2]

Arthur Schopenhauer, a 19th-century German philosopher, said that truth passes through three stages before it's recognized as such. In the first stage, it's *ridiculed;* in the second, it's *opposed;* and in the third, it's regarded as self-evident.[3] For each one of us, our assessment of the truth has to be based on our own experience, not on what someone else tells us, or "medical proof." The experience of a client named Vera best explains this point.

Vera was scheduled for bunion surgery when she came to see me at the urging of a friend. The joint of the big toe was almost perpendicular to the rest of her left foot, and she was in severe pain. Despite protests from her husband, who thought that it was *ridiculous* for her to see a holistic physician instead of following the advice of the orthopedic surgeon, she made an appointment.

After two sessions, in which the subconscious emotional patterns of denied frustration and anger were revealed, Vera's toe visibly began to straighten and the pain greatly diminished. She was very excited about the change, which she shared with the orthopedist when she called to cancel the surgery. He *opposed* her decision, telling her it was impossible to heal bunions without surgery. He warned that she would regret it later. After seeing me once a week for three months and following the Five Basics for Optimal Health (which are explained in Chapter 28), Vera found that her toe was completely straightened.[4]

It's limiting beliefs that equate symptoms with weakness, rather than viewing them as a "message" or "gift" from the body. Often people allow symptoms to define who they are. When peering through the darkness of pain and suffering, they see *anything but* their spirit of pure love.

Defying the Odds

Tom is 59 years young and lives in Ontario, Canada. During a recent healing crisis, he chose not to let the pain and suffering he was experiencing determine the course of his life, and he made a conscious decision to defy the odds:

> I was rushed to the hospital on April 13, 2009, diagnosed with kidney failure. Following numerous tests conducted while I was in the hospital, I also was informed that I had an aortic aneurysm, a ballooning in the main artery of the heart. The doctors all said I would have to begin kidney dialysis immediately, and they warned that the aneurysm could burst at any time, ending my life.
>
> While lying in the hospital bed, I decided that the script of my life depicted by the doctors wasn't going to be the story of my life. I determined I would fight back, win, take charge of my own destiny, and ultimately become an inspiration to others. The odds were against me—I was 100 pounds overweight, had been a heavy smoker for 45 years, and drank numerous cups of coffee every day. As a successful entrepreneur, I also worked long hours. But faced with the prospect of my life coming to a premature end, I decided to change! I lost 75 pounds; quit smoking; cut out

all coffee; switched my work schedule to part-time; and started and stuck to a healthy, low-sodium eating plan.

When I got out of the hospital, I pursued alternative medicine. With the guidance and support of my wife, I discovered a whole new world that had the potential to help me heal. I surrounded myself with positive, educated, and enthusiastic people; and began an entirely new healing regimen. I saw an acupuncturist and master herbalist every week. I've also had the privilege of speaking with a renowned intuitive. Along with the help of these wonderful people, I was referred to Dr. Darren Weissman, who helped me understand the body, mind, and spirit connection to the symptoms I was experiencing. Working with Dr. Weissman helped me find a place of confidence, security, and control in every aspect of my life. I have never felt more alive than I do now.

I am feeling 100 percent better, and my body is getting stronger every day. More than four months later, I have never needed kidney dialysis, nor was it necessary to have the aneurysm removed. I am very grateful for the people who helped me turn my life around; and I am especially thankful for the encouragement of my wife, son, and daughter, who have never let me give up and have encouraged me every step of the way. Infinite Love & Gratitude![5]

The journey of your spirit is to reconnect with the power of Infinite Love & Gratitude. *Infinite* means "the universe," or "one-verse," which has no beginning or end. *Love* is the universal power that propels all of life, fueling your will and enabling you to grow as a result of challenges.[6] *Gratitude* empowers you to move through life with purpose—with this feeling, you recognize the value of any experience as an opportunity, rather than being a victim of circumstances.[7] Gratitude is love in action; it paves the path to inner peace with light. When you're shining, your light reflects on others, illuminating the way for them to know their own potential for peace.

⊕⊕⊕　⊕⊕⊕

CHAPTER 5

Preparing the
Road to Peace

"Our lives become more peaceful when we stop interpreting everything that happens to us, and instead, experience everything that happens to us—no matter what its appearance—as a blessing in disguise."

— Gerald G. Jampolsky, M.D., and Diane V. Cirincione, Ph.D.

Transformation begins when you love yourself unconditionally, when you're willing to completely embrace who you are right now—embracing whatever you're experiencing, and believing in your ability and power to move through it. Society conditions most of us to equate self-love with vanity, self-indulgence, selfishness, or self-centeredness. The truth is, however, acts of vanity, indulgence, and selfishness are often the masks we wear to cover up the fear, anger, resentment, sadness, lack of control, and pain we face in daily life. When we stay in the moment, as Marianne Williamson teaches, healing begins. She says, "Healing occurs in the present, not the past. We are not held back by the love we didn't receive in the past, but by the love we're not extending in the present. . . . As we love, we shall be released from pain . . ."[1]

To love yourself unconditionally doesn't mean you'll *never* feel pain, sadness, frustration, anger, fear, vulnerability, or guilt. Loving yourself *allows* you to embrace those experiences and feelings—to view them as a blessing.

Kally's Experience

Kally is a stay-at-home mom with seven children. She home-schools her youngest kids. She is also a Certified LifeLine Practitioner (CLP). At the age of 19, her eldest son was the youngest person to take and pass the CLP exam.

In April of 2009, Kally's mother, Barbara, became gravely ill. The session that Kally conducted with The LifeLine Technique changed the course of her family's life:

> After experiencing chest pains, my mother was airlifted to a hospital in Arizona with respiratory failure. She was immediately placed on a ventilator, which was breathing for her. She was diagnosed with congestive heart failure, and she also had acute water retention. The doctors said the prognosis was poor.
>
> I called Darren for encouragement, and he reaffirmed my intuitive feeling that my mother was experiencing multiple layers of a broken heart. I knew that to truly heal, she would need to breathe on her own and get off the ventilator. Because I had previously conducted sessions with The LifeLine Technique on my mother, I knew she would want my assistance; and one of my sisters, Kristi, served as her surrogate for the session.
>
> Each painful experience showed up as another layer of a broken heart that had never been acknowledged or expressed. I know it was no coincidence that our mother's body was retaining water, and the emotions associated with the Water element (the kidney and bladder meridians in Chinese medicine) came up during the session. Water has to do with change, transition, and the ability to go with the flow. I harmonized these experiences and emotions with Infinite Love & Gratitude. Our mother slept

deeply after the session. A few hours after she woke up, the doctors took her off the ventilator.

The next day when I felt that our mother was comfortable and out of crisis, Kristi and I discussed with her the issues that came up during the session. Our mother previously had never talked about the death of her father, and she always seemed to be holding back her feelings; she never hugged me or my siblings. However, when I told her about the session, she opened up for the first time:

> *My father was killed in a small plane crash. Later we learned that there was water in the plane's gas line and that's what caused the crash. When I arrived home, I was drinking water when I learned that my father had been killed, and I think I may have choked. The next day I had to attend school. I remember all the kids were pointing at me, talking about me because they knew about my father, but no one said a word to me. . . . I'll never forget how I had to return to school as soon as his funeral service ended. . . .*

After she shared her story, our mother cried deeply. I could feel her letting go. For the first time, I knew she had peace of mind. Following the session with The LifeLine Technique, her body was able to release 30 pounds of water fairly quickly. Most important, our mother was happier than I'd ever seen her; she had the most beautiful smile! I am so proud that she chose to face her fear and live!

Our mom reached out to give us hugs and kisses whenever we visited her hospital room after that. Although the process of healing was slow while she was in the hospital, her spirit continued to thrive![2]

One of the essential aspects of healing is recognizing the interconnection between our experiences and the state of our lives. As David Hawkins writes in *Power vs. Force,* "our decisions ripple through the universe of consciousness to affect the lives of all."[3]

It's Not a Conscious Choice

No one ever consciously chooses illness or tormenting, irritating, or frightening experiences. However, the reality is that they are the fuel for healing and transformation. A developing chick cracks its shell when it grows too large to remain inside. The process of hatching—pecking its way through the protective covering, pushing its beak, head, and wings through the shell—is a painful and sometimes arduous struggle to awaken to its new reality: the life of a chicken. The protective cover that enshrouds us in the developing stages of our spirit is constructed by the subconscious mind. Every time we feel hurt, troubled, alarmed, or intimidated, it is a signal that we're ready to crack the next layer of the shell.

Painful, scary, or challenging emotions and experiences are synonymous with growing pains. When these pains, or symptoms, are felt, they're meant to be *experienced* with courage and faith so that we can crack the shell of the smaller self and awaken to an intentional life—the predominance of the mind over matter and the power to both experience and create our reality.

No matter what your age or state in life, you're a spiritual being on an evolutionary journey in an interdependent and holographic universe.

Are you ready to crack your shell? Are you willing to be much more than your conscious mind is perceiving? Symptoms and stress are the beacons, or signals, from the subconscious mind letting you know that you now have the ability to make a choice to change your reality . . . no matter what you or others perceive your reality to be. Willingness to change, in essence, is your path to inner peace.

⊕⊕⊕　⊕⊕⊕

CHAPTER 6

The Path to Peace

"I do not want the peace that passeth understanding.
I want the understanding which bringeth peace."

— Helen Keller

As you hold this book in your hand, you're standing at the precipice of quantum change. Who you are matters and will have an impact on the world that you're a part of and are creating. Your contribution is uniquely yours, as famed American choreographer and dancer Martha Graham pointed out:

> There is only one of you in all time, this expression is unique, and if you block it, it will never exist through any other medium; and be lost. The world will not have it. It's not your business to determine how good it is, not how it compares with other expression. It's your business to keep it yours clearly and directly, to keep the channel open . . .[1]

Many people, just like you, are standing on this precipice. They represent a community of like-minded, empowered souls who are taking a stand to choose love in the face of fear.

I want to share the healing journey of my dear friend and colleague Madge Bares, whose profound courage and passion has taught me how, as Martha Graham noted, to keep the channel of Infinite Love & Gratitude open, regardless of circumstances.

On June 27, 2007, my home telephone rang at about 6:30 A.M. My wife, Sarit, answered. I heard her gasp as she listened. Before I could ask her what was going on, she handed me the phone. Choking with tears, Madge shared the worst news I could have ever imagined: her son, Kylen, had been killed by a drunk driver.

In that moment, it was hard to even fathom, especially as a parent, how anyone could possibly pick up the pieces to begin to take a baby step through what I knew was the darkest night for Madge; her husband, Steve; and their daughter, Audra. As both her friend and mentor, I wasn't completely sure whether I had the tools or strategies to help her transform this tragic and unjust experience into anything purposeful or meaningful. As I was to learn over the next two years, there are no guidelines or rules to follow. I just used the power of Infinite Love & Gratitude to guide us. The following is Madge's account of her transformation:

In 2005, when I sat in the front row at The LifeLine Technique Training Program in Memphis, Tennessee, I had no idea that I would be learning the infinitely powerful tools needed to guide me through the most challenging ordeal of my life . . . the sudden death of my beautiful 22-year-old son, Kylen, two years later. Nor could I have ever fathomed that what I thought was merely a healing "technique" would fuel a personal journey from devastating loss to touching the quantum field spoken of by Rumi—which has allowed me to discover the limitless potential of the human soul to connect to everything and everyone. I only know that when I read the words *We Are All One* above the Infinite Love & Gratitude "hand sign" at the end of Darren's presentation, somewhere deep in my heart I understood the truth of this statement, and I *knew* that I had to learn this work.

On June 27, 2007, about 2 A.M., my husband and I were startled out of sleep by pounding at our front door. My son's best friend, David; David's mother; and another one of my son's close friends, Mike, stepped into our dimly lit living room. David began to stammer out the terrible news that Kylen had been killed by a drunk driver only an hour before. The words crushed me, like a giant meteor striking Mother Earth, and all life, as I had ever known it, went suddenly dark and still.

Darren's first LifeLine session with me toward finding light again was on the phone that morning when I called him at 6:30. I remember feeling the depth of his empathy as we cried together, and the strength of his love pouring from his heart, through the stabilizing sound of his voice: *"Infinite Love & Gratitude, Infinite Love & Gratitude, Infinite Love & Gratitude."*

That power carried me through the agonizing days leading up to the funeral, where I was able to stand in front of hundreds of mourning friends and family, telling stories about Kylen and sharing one of the basic principles of The LifeLine Technique philosophy: although we did not choose this tragedy, we could choose how to *respond* to it and live lives of service to each other, as Kylen had done for so many. I concluded my remarks by holding my hand up with the Infinite Love & Gratitude sign, directing it to Kylen's grieving friends as a sign of love—from him to them, and between all of us.

Among the friends who packed the chapel were members of my LifeLine "family," including Darren, Jeri Love, and Dan Ohlman, who all flew in from Chicago. They stayed the weekend, offering LifeLine sessions and immeasurable comfort to my family. I somehow knew that I was being "held together" by the presence of these dear friends, who believed beyond all doubt that Kylen's soul was very much alive and among us. Besides being very worried about how my husband and daughter would get through this, my all-consuming question concerned how to maintain a connection with my son, although I did not know how it would manifest. I was desperate to ensure that he was happy and at peace, that he knew how much I loved him, and that he would forever be in my heart and a part of my life.

The first six months after Kylen's death were difficult beyond description. But I can't imagine navigating through them without the daily phone calls from my LifeLine family. Sometimes conducting sessions on myself brought out extraordinary moments of clarity where I strongly felt Kylen's presence and knew that feelings of calm would someday be restored to my heart and my home. But on tough days, I sat on my bed, clutching Kylen's sweatshirt, rocking back and forth and crying or sometimes screaming, "Infinite Love & Gratitude!" over and over until the nauseating wave of sorrow receded. This excruciating period of my life taught me firsthand the fullest meaning of the word *LifeLine*.

By mid-January, our family was still recovering from the gauntlet of our first holidays, and my birthday, without Kylen. I made a conscious decision to do my best to get back into my life, and I traveled to Long Beach, California, to join the team assisting Darren at The LifeLine Technique Training Program. Honestly, I was feeling anything but thankful, peaceful, or joyful. But while observing Darren teach the training the first morning, I physically felt Kylen's life force. It literally "tapped" me on my left shoulder. Kylen's voice was clear: "Mom, it's *time* to deal with this grief." Despite a full and intense day of teaching, Darren agreed to conduct a LifeLine session with me.

I called the grief "the abyss." I told Darren that I had "walked" around the rim many times but was terrified to look into the complete blackness that consumed all light.

Darren didn't flinch. He said we were going "through" it and assured me that he wouldn't let me fall. Incredibly, the darkest point of the abyss became a portal to what might best be described as "the field," or "heaven," where Kylen's spirit invited us to experience his world of blissful peace and universal love. It was as infinitely mind-expanding as it was healing . . . a moment that changed my life forever.

Looking back a year later, I'm still in complete awe of the capacity of this brilliant quantum-healing technology to bridge the gap from the depths of mind-numbing grief to true spiritual joy. I have spent this past year studying, meditating, experimenting, making "mistakes" and learning from them, and consulting intuitives. I have directly asked Kylen (he shakes my left shoulder for "yes") to help me learn ways to maintain this connection between both worlds, which both strengthens my ties with my son and helps me find answers for the clients I serve.

The core foundation for this often tedious and often painful work has been Darren's continual willingness to provide support by conducting LifeLine sessions, which has accelerated my personal growth to a phenomenal level.

For example, months after my son's death, I went through a period of intense anger. I did not want to forgive the young woman whose drunken driving was responsible for Kylen's death. In fact, I could not wait for her to go to jail. The catalyst for my having the opportunity to break through this anger was the letter my husband wrote to the judge about what Kylen's loss meant to our family:

> *Your Honor:*
>
> *My name is Steve Bares, and I am the father of Kylen Bares. Thank you for listening to our family and for reading all the letters that were written to you by our friends and members of the community.*
>
> *On April 6, 1985, my son was placed in my arms for the first time, just minutes after he took his first breath. It was my 28th birthday, and he was a precious gift, his face so flawless, his skin soft, and I whispered, "I love you, son," for the first time.*
>
> *On the evening of June 26, 2007, my 22-year-old son and I sat at the kitchen table, spoke about the day's activities and next day's plans, and said "I love you" as he left the house.*
>
> *On June 27, 2007, I entered the county morgue and was shown a picture of my beautiful, lifeless son. This time his face was not flawless; his skin appeared cold, and I whispered, "I love you, son," for the last time.*
>
> *I have tried to find words that describe how my son's death has impacted my life; but there are no adequate words to describe the pain, anger, and despair that I've felt from that day. I have trouble finding joy in the simple pleasures of life. Being "happy" doesn't seem "right" anymore. It's like having*

*a terrible cold that numbs the mind and dims the senses,
and then there are moments when the feeling of despair is so
overwhelming, it literally takes my breath away. I never know
what is going to trigger a memory. And while the memories of
Kylen are so many, with them comes the realization that he
is gone. And each time that his death hits my heart, it opens
the wound and, occasionally, dark black clouds come. A huge
part of me died along with Kylen. . . .*

Darren conducted a LifeLine session with me, reading aloud
my husband's letter, line by line, harmonizing the pain with
Infinite Love & Gratitude. By the end of that exquisite session,
my frozen, shattered heart, which had never fully opened in this
lifetime, energetically melted, enabling me to process the sacred
contract of the intertwined fate that my family shared with the
young woman who was charged with causing the fatal accident. As
a consequence, I was able to unconditionally accept her apology
to our family at the sentencing hearing several weeks later.

The greatest gift that Kylen has given me through the vehicle
of LifeLine and the unbelievably kind and beautiful people who
practice it is the breakthrough to the real *Me*—the eternal, infinitely powerful soul who is, and always has been, unquestionably
loved and connected to all of life. Until recently, no matter how
many books I read, those deeply rooted feelings of self-doubt and
unworthiness always kept the illusion of separation alive . . . for
subconscious reasons of protection, of course! Paradoxically, it
was my role as a determined, grief-stricken mother that drove me
to find the Truth that life is so much more than we ever imagined
it could be, far beyond the roles we play.

From that higher "observation tower" of infinite possibilities,
I've noticed an inner peacefulness and calm *knowing* that all
is well, despite outer circumstances. I'm also able to focus for
longer periods of time; to love myself, love others, and allow
others to love me; to feel greater compassion for all humanity;
to hold an unquestioned belief that all people are "wired" to
receive intuitive information and guidance; and to feel even
more passionate about my life's work as a Certified LifeLine

Practitioner. Even physically, my body is 20 pounds lighter, gives me great energy, and is happy to run two miles every day.

If I had to sum up my feelings about the power of The LifeLine Technique to completely change one's emotional, biochemical, structural, and spiritual life, I'd say that my own experience of moving from intense personal tragedy to experiencing authentic joy in a year and a half is no less than miraculous. I'm not saying that I don't still miss seeing and hugging my son absolutely every day. That kind of love is intrinsic to physical and emotional reality here in "Earth School"; that will never go away, nor do I wish it to. But I can look at Kylen's baby pictures now and smile with fond memories, and sing his favorite song by Nickel Creek as I play his guitar (these were portals in sessions with Darren).

I know that the power of Infinite Love & Gratitude can heal the entire planet . . . when individuals, one by one, plug into the "LifeLine" and discover that we are never alone or separate— that, indeed, *"we are all One!"*[2]

We may never be able to get to a place where sorrow and pain don't reside. It's not realistic. When we lose someone we love, the enormity of the loss is so complicated and oppressive that it's not something that can be put into perspective without Herculean effort and intense internal battles.[3] To achieve the "spiritual joy" that Madge professed required "tedious and often painful work." In the face of unbearable sorrow, Madge showed us the way— acceptance with Infinite Love & Gratitude. Her heart opened to infinite possibilities and a bond with her son that she could have never before fathomed.

The LifeLine Technique is the bridge through fear, pain, and suffering. It helps you discover the love in your heart that's waiting and ready to blossom. Despite the inevitable fears associated with change, it's the only path to healing. It requires that you liberate your old identity of being afraid, guilty, ashamed, or helpless and open your life and heart to the possibility of who you can become. To do that, as taught by Gerald Jampolsky, M.D., in his book *Love Is Letting Go of Fear*, you must retrain your mind by taking responsibility for your choices and subsequent actions.[4]

During one of the most difficult and painful periods of his political career, then–Presidential candidate Barack Obama gave a speech in 2008 that marked the redetermination of his will to become the 44th President of the United States. "Yes, we can!" he declared on a chilly January night in New Hampshire, and the country and the world believed him.

The moment you set the intention and vision for yourself—allowing yourself to see and feel the value of change—your mind, as well as every nerve and fiber of your being, will immediately orient itself toward helping you manifest your intention.[5] Yes, *you* can!

⊕⊕⊕ ⊕⊕⊕

CHAPTER 7

Living in the Now

*". . . the way of peace is the way of love. Love is
the greatest power on earth. It conquers all things."*

— Peace Pilgrim

At every Hay House "I Can Do It!" conference, a group of
Certified LifeLine Practitioners and I offer sessions with The
LifeLine Technique at my booth in the vendors' section of the
conference hall. During one such event in Las Vegas, there were
lines of people waiting a couple of hours to receive a session, and
I noticed out of the corner of my eye a Tibetan Buddhist monk
dressed in a flowing saffron robe and crimson sash. She watched
me as I conducted a session with The LifeLine Technique, and
when I finished, she approached me.

"Do you know what that hand symbol represents?" she asked,
pointing to one of The LifeLine Technique banners with a picture
of the logo.

Although of course I knew what the "I love you" hand mode
meant, I was curious about her interpretation. "What does it mean
to you?" I inquired.

"It's the mudra of Yamantaka."

As I learned during our subsequent 20-minute conversation, Yamantaka is the Sanskrit name for a Mahayana Buddhist deity. *Yama* is the god of death, and *antaka* means "terminator." Yamantaka's name is literally defined as "the slayer of death."[1] Yamantaka represents the goal of the Buddhist practitioner's journey to enlightenment, or the journey to awaken. There are two aspects to death, the monk said—the death of the physical body and the death of ignorance of the true nature of reality.

I felt a chill move from my head to my toes as she explained her beliefs to me. It was the vibration of resonance, which reaffirms something I already believe to be true. I both knew and had experienced the power of the "I love you" hand mudra; I had already witnessed the life-changing results of the universal healing frequency of Infinite Love & Gratitude. The conversation with the monk reaffirmed to me that The LifeLine Technique sessions are a journey to enlightenment, to awaken to the true nature of the reality of your life.

Enlightenment represents the oneness of everything and everyone. It enables you to see past the physical identity into the realm of the nonphysical. Enlightenment recognizes the interconnection of all things and brings to light the bridge of energy between the visible and invisible worlds.

At the core of all matter is energy. It's what you focus your energy on that turns to matter (representing what *matters* to you). Enlightenment occurs when what once mattered now is viewed in divine right order and timing. One doesn't need to die to reach enlightenment. By bridging the gap between the conscious and subconscious minds, you're able to view your life from a heightened perspective, rather than through the reactive projections of the subconscious. Once the gap of consciousness is bridged, the mind is one . . . a super-conscious mind of enlightenment.

Thinking about the image of Yamantaka, I later realized that this mudra transcends cultural boundaries and has many different meanings. Upon further exploration, I learned that the "I love you" hand signal is similar to the *Karana* mudra common to Buddhist deities of many different sects. I recalled seeing pictures of Jesus Christ displaying the "I love you" mudra. It's also used by our friendly, neighborhood superhero Spider-Man to dispense webs to catch bad guys.

Although I don't know this to be the intention of the original comic strip or the films, I see Spider-Man as a metaphor for the subconscious mind, spinning a web around what we perceive to be the darkness in our lives (crooks, thieves, and evildoers) . . . that space where a gap of consciousness exists. Like a caterpillar in a chrysalis, we're bound in a cocoon until we're ready to assume our true identity—the butterfly—and create a new reality for our lives.

Embracing the Power of Love

The following experience from Lucinda, who lives in Florida, demonstrates how changing your thoughts (the death of ignorance) and embracing the transformative power of self-love can save your life:

> My sister had been diagnosed with cancer of the vulva and was constantly struggling with many negative thoughts about her health, her marriage, her job, and so on. She saw nothing good on the horizon. It hurt me to see her suffering like this because she had been the life of any gathering and a ray of sunshine to everyone who knew her. To think of losing her was more than I could stand. I knew that if she didn't take some action to save herself, the outcome would not be good.
>
> I hoped that if she changed her thinking, it would save her life. I told her about Louise Hay's book *You Can Heal Your Life.* But I knew that if I could get her to go to the "I Can Do It!" conference, she would feel the same positive energy both my mother and I did when we were in Las Vegas. I was sure that someone would say something that would resonate with her, and she would have an awakening. To my joy and delight, she agreed to attend.

The Saturday of the conference, my sister purchased a copy of *You Can Heal Your Life.* My mother and I waited in line with her to have Louise Hay sign her book. I could see the shift had started. On the last day of the conference, my sister felt compelled to go back and ask Louise about how she had been able to overcome cancer. She knew this would be her last opportunity to speak with her and hopefully get some answers. Louise advised my sister to do a lot of mirror work—to look in the mirror and say aloud, "I love you unconditionally." And then she did the most incredible thing—she momentarily excused herself to the people in line still waiting, took my sister by the hand, and walked her over to the LifeLine booth. Louise asked one of the practitioners to take care of my sister and then turned to her and said, "These people can help you get started." We were elated, and hopeful for the possibilities for my precious little sister.

She met a very caring and compassionate being of light, Madge Bares, who is a Certified LifeLine Practitioner. At that time, my sister was in so much pain that she could barely breathe, and her thoughts were all over the place. None of us knew what to expect. Madge conducted a LifeLine session with her that took at least 45 minutes.

As soon as the session ended, we had to take my sister to the airport to catch her flight home. She was physically ill, and she said she felt faint. I know now that she was in the process of bridging the gap between her conscious and subconscious minds . . . her subconscious mind began to let go of the subconscious identity that was no longer serving her. Even though she felt ill, my sister told us that she felt a deep sense of peace, freedom, and relief. *Wow!*

My sister had one more session with Madge over the telephone. Three months later, the oncologist told her the cancer was gone! It has now been close to two years, and my sister remains cancer free. My mother and I have both since learned The LifeLine Technique, and we use it on ourselves and others. I am truly grateful to Louise Hay for throwing my sister and my family a LifeLine![2]

Change Your Game

"A move of even one pawn on the chessboard completely changes the game," Dr. Hawkins wrote in *Power vs. Force*. "Every detail of the belief system that we hold has consequences for better or worse. It's for this reason that there's no such thing as an incurable or hopeless condition—somewhere, at some time, somebody has recovered from it."[3]

Ultimately, the most important thing in life isn't what happens to us. Rather, it is how we *choose* to respond to our experiences. Change your game. Be open to the fact that the moment you decide your life will change, you have the power to transform the impossible into the possible. Regardless of your circumstances, if this is your choice, then your evolutionary journey has already begun!

Take a deep breath and say aloud to yourself: "I have the power to choose how I respond to my life's experiences." The choices you make represent your will—the engine that drives the spirit. Therefore, love is the *only* choice; and love in action is practiced as acceptance, forgiveness, gratitude, and compassion.

⊕⊕⊕ ⊕⊕⊕

CHAPTER 8

To Know What
We Know

"We have as a society come to the end of our journey in Newtonian medicine, a perspective that looks at the body more like a bag of organs and bones than a miracle of animation; that focuses on illness rather than optimizing health. . . . Einstein was right—energy is all there is. . . . You change your energy and, over time, your body has to respond."

— Christiane Northrup, M.D.

Nicolaus Copernicus was an astronomer and mathematician who passionately believed that the earth rotated on an axis while simultaneously moving around the sun. His work was later accepted by his peers and became the basis for modern-day astronomy. However, for most of Copernicus's life, the Catholic Church vehemently opposed his views. Nonetheless, he didn't let the lack of scientific documentation or the denunciations of his spiritual perspective change his mind. A quote attributed to Confucius by Henry David Thoreau echoes this understanding of the universe: "To know that we know what we know, and to know that we do not know what we do not know, that is true knowledge."[1]

Like Copernicus's views of astronomy during the 16th century, The LifeLine Technique is a new paradigm of thinking, feeling, choosing, and taking action for the 21st century. It's based upon a profound understanding of the subconscious mind's function and the fundamental principle that every cell in the body and every relationship in life is intelligently designed to heal, completely regenerate, and be whole.

The function of the subconscious mind is simultaneously miraculous and mysterious; and it's a field of study that, despite its deep roots, is still not widely understood. While some modern-day neuroscientists describe the subconscious as an "active and independent guide to behaviour," they also believe there's no *reliable* way to distinguish between the conscious and subconscious thought processes.[2]

However, the work of conscious visionaries, such as theoretical quantum physicist Amit Goswami, Ph.D., and cellular biologist Bruce Lipton, Ph.D., challenges so-called established scientific theories about the power of mind over matter. Their work prompts us all to completely reevaluate life as we know it. As a result, they have helped make it possible for anyone and everyone to understand the frontier of the subconscious mind and the vast opportunities this awareness affords us.

I'd like to take a moment to focus on Dr. Lipton's work, which is documented in his best-selling book *The Biology of Belief*. His work helped reaffirm my understanding of the dominant nature of the subconscious mind as taught in The LifeLine Technique Training Program.

We're the "masters of our fate, not victims of our genes," Dr. Lipton wrote. "The biggest impediments" to achieving our hopes and dreams "are the limitations programmed into the subconscious. These limitations not only influence our behavior, they can also play a major role in determining our physiology and health." He further explains: "We have the capacity to consciously evaluate our responses to environmental stimuli and change old responses any time we desire . . . once we deal with the powerful subconscious mind.[3]

To further demonstrate his point, Dr. Lipton wrote about the *placebo effect,* which he said is taught as part of the traditional medical-school curricula. One-third of all medical healings, he wrote, including surgery, are the result of the placebo effect, instead of medical intervention.[4] This means that a patient taking a sugar pill under the assumption that it would "cure" the condition experienced significant change. The same thing occurred when patients were told they had surgery when in fact no procedure had been done.[5]

Dr. Lipton wrote that the majority of medical doctors don't recognize the significance of the placebo effect. However, we know from quantum physics that we see what we believe. More than likely, the belief that "harnessing the power of your mind can be *more* effective than the drugs you have been programmed to believe you need . . . [and that] energy is a *more* efficient means of affecting matter than chemicals"[6] is too scary or challenging for most in the medical establishment to accept.

The journey that I'm about to share with you involves Diane, a Certified LifeLine Practitioner based in Adelaide, South Australia, and her client Annie. Diane began reading *The Power of Infinite Love & Gratitude* while riding in a car with her husband, Robert. They were traveling to Melbourne from their home in Adelaide. Halfway through the book, she later told me, she turned to Robert and declared, "I've got to go to the States to meet this man."

I've since gotten to know Diane, and she is a Goddess of light and love. She's the facilitator of life-transforming Goddess Within workshops. Her passion and determination to spread the power of Infinite Love & Gratitude resulted in the first LifeLine Technique training in Australia, in March 2009. Annie's experience is indicative of the challenges many people with health imbalances are struggling with today.

Before someone misconstrues my intentions, I want to say up front that Western emergency medicine is the finest in the world. Medication in life-threatening situations is *absolutely essential.* My grandfather was a pharmacist, and I know that his work saved lives. However, what concerns me—what causes suffering under the name of "side effects" for millions of people—is the Newtonian medical model that, in my opinion, defaults to the simplest of solutions when an answer isn't immediately obvious: "Take this pill."

"Take this pill" is questionable advice when the power of the mind, even as taught in medical school, actually works.[7] Some people will argue that there's not enough evidence for "trusting the mind" to risk people's lives. But I believe there's much more evidence on the *other* side of this equation, as demonstrated by Diane and Annie's experience:

> **Diane:** For nine years, my eyes had been "speaking to me" with what the doctor diagnosed as *exophthalmos,* a painful disorder that causes the eyes to bulge. I was enormously distressed, acutely embarrassed, and always in excruciating pain. But after the sessions I received at The LifeLine Technique training with Madge Bares, a Certified LifeLine Practitioner, my eyes were flat! When I got home, I immediately began looking for people with whom to share the work and offer sessions.
>
> Since then, I've conducted sessions on untold numbers of people and have had the opportunity to witness absolute miracles. One of them was Annie. I heard from a mutual friend that she'd been bedridden for several years. I immediately sent an e-mail to Annie offering to work with her for free because I was still learning. . . .[8]
>
> **Annie:** Before meeting Diane, I was primarily confined to bed, suffering from a host of approximately 30 symptoms. These ranged from extreme pain, vertigo, and tinnitus to the deepest depths of morbid depression. I was living in fear that any undue movement, strain, or stress would cause another bout of unbearable symptoms. I felt jealous when I saw people walking down the street or shopping, or sitting in a café chatting happily, and taking their good health or ability to move around at will for granted.

In 2001, I was diagnosed with having an overactive thyroid and put on thyroid hormone replacement for 18 months. Although the decision to take medication was against all of my principles—I didn't even take aspirin—I was assured that it would only be temporary. One morning, the top half of my body felt as if it had exploded. This was followed by full-blown panic attacks . . . every morning and every night, every day for weeks on end. Each panic attack felt like a systemic, overwhelming, all-encompassing fear. My body was in total shock; I felt as if I was about to die and there was nothing that I could do about it.

I changed doctors. I spent whole days in hospital emergency rooms having every imaginable test—ECGs, x-rays, CAT scans, et cetera, ad nauseam. The result was always the same: "We don't know what is wrong." Finally, the doctor prescribed another drug—a tranquilizer. He recommended benzodiazepine, which has been found to cause severe and prolonged disruption of the brain's neurotransmitters, affecting every part of the body. Years later "benzos" in fatal combination with narcotic sleeping aids were involved in the death of the actor Heath Ledger, according to the New York City medical examiner's report.

I argued with my doctor about the side effects and dependency. However, he promised the dosage was too small for me to become dependent, and he said when the time came for me to stop taking the drugs, he would help me. Unfortunately, neither of his statements was true.

A year after taking the first tranquilizer, I discovered that I had been misdiagnosed. Instead of having an overactive thyroid, I actually had adrenal exhaustion due to prolonged stress (I was a government consultant), and an *underactive* thyroid. The panic attacks stemmed from the adrenal failure, most likely triggered by the first medication.

I decided to stop taking the tranquilizer on Christmas Day 2005. Immediately, I fell into what is called "benzo withdrawal syndrome," with its myriad prolonged and severe symptoms, including nausea, constipation, diarrhea, distorted vision, dizziness, uncontrolled shaking, tight chest, ringing in the ears, headaches, sore eyes, tight band around the head, and rubbery legs.

When I arrived at my first meeting with Diane, I was helped into the room where she was conducting the session with The LifeLine Technique. Sixty minutes later, I was able to walk out unaided. After being practically bedridden for several years, this was a miracle in itself! After each session, I felt stronger and healthier.

My last session was the best testament of all. I was in full-blown benzo withdrawal on that day, but after having great results from my first two sessions (which had the effect of peeling back the layers, and I knew I still had more to go), I was determined to get to Diane for a session. I struggled in with about 20 symptoms and walked out about an hour later feeling amazing.

On the way home, my husband and I stopped off at the Grange Jetty Kiosk and reveled in the beautiful ocean views. For the first time, I was no longer jealous of those other people outside enjoying the day. I felt at peace. It was "me" this time chatting happily in a café, but unlike before, not taking my health for granted—accepting it with "Infinite Love & Gratitude."[9]

The Catalyst for Transformation

Love unlocks the heart, and gratitude bathes it with the light of clarity. Together, Infinite Love & Gratitude are catalysts for extraordinary transformation, setting your spirit free. The freedom of your spirit, no matter what the circumstances, is the gateway for inner peace. Louise Hay, the matriarch of the world's self-help revolution, says: "I now rejoice whenever I see another portion of the dark side of myself. I know that it means that I am ready to let go of something that has been hindering my life. I say aloud, 'Thank you for showing me this, so I can heal it and move on.'"[10]

It's not until the subconscious is made conscious—seeing the dark side, experiencing, like Annie, myriad competing symptoms—that you're able to choose or take action based on what you're truly experiencing in any given moment.

The Health Revolution of the 21st Century

What if you could—like a diamond forged through heat and pressure—transform the most painful, scary, or stressful experience in your life into one that is meaningful, courageous, and inspiring, as Annie did? What if you were given the tools to tap into and manifest the true power that exists within you—the power to shine? Are you ready to discover *your* brilliant path to peace?

If you have a background in *kinesiology,* a system that uses muscle testing, you'll have an easy time appreciating the logical foundation and structure of The LifeLine Technique. If you don't have such a background, you'll be learning to use a new instrument in Part II. This can take time and requires patience, persistence, and passion. But I promise you, you can learn it and use it to transform your life. I have DVDs available that will help support you in this process of mastering muscle-reflex testing. There is also a cadre of Certified LifeLine Practitioners who have been specially trained to help you learn how to use the 1-2-3 PLAN of The LifeLine Technique (see the Information and Resources section in the back of the book). They're as passionate as I am about sharing the power of Infinite Love & Gratitude.

Master the Art of Living

Learning The LifeLine Technique is akin to mastering an art form. Every artistic endeavor, from writing to painting, requires basic skills. Once you master the basics, your art will naturally evolve from your own volition, interests, and passion. Keep in mind, even Picasso started with a pencil, and he spent a lot of time practicing! I urge you to take your time, and with complete acceptance of the journey, study Part II and practice with the intention that you're already a master of The LifeLine Technique. *Feel* it in your heart!

⊕⊕⊕ ⊕⊕⊕

PART II

Interpreting the Code
of Your Mind

*"The way of the heart leads to peace.
Peace in turn, opens the heart."*

— Anodea Judith

Introduction to Part II

It's as Easy as 1-2-3!

More than 25 years ago, in the definitive mind-body healing classic *You Can Heal Your Life*, Louise L. Hay wrote: "The only thing we are ever dealing with is a thought, and a thought can be changed."[1] The pioneering work of other conscious visionaries—such as Deepak Chopra, Masaru Emoto, Candace Pert, Bruce Lipton, and Gregg Braden—has provided more stepping-stones along the path to peace. Today, we have come to understand that it isn't our *conscious* thoughts that are creating the pain, fear, or stress we experience in our lives, but rather the *subconscious* ones. The challenge has been to find the secret to interpreting the code of the subconscious mind.

Part II contains all of the building blocks necessary to activate and interpret the language of the subconscious mind—learning to use muscle-reflex testing, the Infinite Love & Gratitude Sequence (ILS), and the 1-2-3 PLAN of The LifeLine Technique Flow Chart. I will explain in detail the philosophy and science of each of the 16 steps of The LifeLine Technique Flow Chart and thus provide a clear vision of the "simply intricate" order of the mind and the role it plays in every aspect of life.

Part II is where you'll begin the journey inward to awaken:

- The power to continually upgrade the field of your spirit to live in the now

- The ease of transforming every physical symptom and stressful experience into an intention that genetically aligns the intelligent design of the cells in your body and the relationships of your life, manifesting through thoughts, feelings, and actions

- The ability to create portals that open the divine potential of your mind and body for healing, regeneration, and wholeness

There may be some terms that you have never heard before, or you may not recognize the way in which I'm using them. Please refer to the Glossary in the back of the book if you have any confusion.

As you awaken to the meaning and significance of The LifeLine Technique in all aspects of your life, you'll no longer view tightness in your shoulders, pain in your knee, the stubbing of your toe, a flash of anger at your co-worker, frustration with your boss, and an argument with your significant other or spouse as only annoyances or isolated incidents. Each of those symptoms or stressors has a reactive *subconscious* story that is unique to you.

Revealing yourself as a master of The LifeLine Technique requires a willingness to become a perennial student. Let's begin to build the foundation to unleash the master that already exists within you.

⊕⊕⊕ ⊕⊕⊕

CHAPTER 9

Becoming a Master
of Dialogue

*"Dialogue possesses a remarkable power to effect personal
and spiritual growth and can offer our world perhaps the greatest
means for the healing and further evolution of society."*

— Robert Apatow, Ph.D.

In ancient Greece, people sought opportunities to dialogue as a meaningful, social activity. The primary purpose was to develop an *understanding* of each other. By sharing their thoughts, which were believed to be the speech of the soul, people revealed to each other the *truth* of their lives.[1]

Today, the biggest obstacle to dialogue is language. For example, 你好朋友! 你好吗? 很好, 我希望! If you don't speak or read Mandarin Chinese, these characters won't mean very much to you. However if you do, then you'll recognize: "Hello, friends! How are you? Well, I hope!" Do you speak Spanish? *¡Le deseo Infinito Amor y Gratitud!* Spanish speakers will know that the previous sentence reads: "I wish you Infinite Love & Gratitude!"

As discussed in Part I, the language that your subconscious mind uses to communicate imbalance and disconnection is

59

symptoms and stress. This language is foreign to most of us because we weren't taught to perceive symptoms as a form of communication. However, learning this language and using The LifeLine Technique to decode it is the key to health, healing, and living a purposeful life.

If your goal is to become a master of dialogue in order to learn the truth of *your* life, then the primary tools are muscle-reflex testing (MRT), the Infinite Love & Gratitude Sequence (ILS), and the 1-2-3 PLAN of The LifeLine Technique Flow Chart. In this chapter, I'll focus on MRT; the rest of these tools will be explained in detail in subsequent chapters.

A Symptom Decoder

Muscle-reflex testing evaluates the electromagnetic conductivity of the nervous system and how it maintains balance between your internal and external environments. Maintaining balance is a subconscious function; and like the subconscious, MRT is an autonomic, automatic reflex pattern of emotional reaction activated by any one of the senses. Simply seeing a color, smelling a fragrance, or being touched can activate this automatic type of reflex.

Both MRT and The LifeLine Technique Flow Chart are used to interpret the code of symptoms and stress. Please remember: *The LifeLine Technique and muscle-reflex testing are not used to diagnose disease, or treat or cure anyone or anything!* "Diagnosis" is part of the paradigm of allopathic (Western) medicine, which has as its primary focus the treatment of disease or the eradication of symptoms. Medical doctors use diagnostic tools, such as blood tests or urinalysis, to determine whether there's *diagnosable dysfunction* in the body. Based on their interpretation of the results of the tests, they then make diagnoses. Most often they prescribe pharmaceutical medication or surgery to treat, suppress, and/or alleviate the symptoms.

Western medicine's approach is based on the belief that the primary causes of symptoms and stress are genetic abnormalities or an external assault of pathogens (viruses, bacteria, fungi, and so forth) that render a person helpless. Most, if not all, of the diseases referenced in the *Merck Manual* (medical doctors' bible) list "idiopathic" as the cause. This is a fancy way of saying that the root cause is unknown.

I want to reaffirm that I believe that in the West we're extremely fortunate to have the best system in the world when it comes to emergency medicine. However, to our peril, today's medical establishment ignores the basic philosophical premise of Hippocrates, the "father of medicine," who foretold and warned against today's "specialized medicine." He believed that the body should be treated as a whole rather than as a series of parts, and recommended creating conditions to foster the body's natural healing capabilities with the proper amount of rest, a good diet, fresh air, and cleanliness.[2] Did he know what he was talking about? You can be the judge—Hippocrates was believed to be at least in his 90s, perhaps more than 100, when he died.

True health is much more than the absence of symptoms or stress in your body or life. It's a state of wholeness where you're able to recognize every experience as meaningful . . . every experience as fuel for the journey you're on. In this state of recognition, acceptance and compassion are born; forgiveness and gratitude are natural states of being. From a state of wholeness, you see yourself as one with the world's intricate order, infinite wisdom, and ongoing process of transformation.

"They Call It a Miracle"

Debbie is a Certified LifeLine Practitioner based in Georgia. She met Paul in May of 2008, just after she completed the second level of The LifeLine Technique training. She asked him if she could practice what she was learning with him, and he agreed. Paul, 50, has given me permission to share his experience:

In 2005, I was diagnosed with a very serious and rare form of cancer. I had both standard and experimental treatments, but all of them failed. Debbie began to work with me frequently— once or twice a week. Quite frankly, I didn't understand the technique or how it worked. My motivation at the time was that I was helping Debbie practice, doing a favor for a friend. I had nothing to lose. She explained to me that The LifeLine Technique couldn't hurt me in any way; at worst, I was being filled with Infinite Love & Gratitude. At no time during our work together did Debbie suggest that I stop any of the treatments or disregard any instructions from the doctor. Her work was complementary to all other treatments.

Debbie told me that physical cancer is always preceded by what she referred to as "emotional cancer," which she said was mutated emotions. During the sessions, emotional cancer was found at my current age; at the ages of 13, 7, and 4; at the moment of my birth; and even at 19 weeks in the womb. It was astounding the number of emotions and traumatic events that were cleared out. At no time during my sessions with Debbie did I feel re-traumatized. Apparently I took all the physical, verbal, and emotional abuse I experienced during my violent childhood and internalized it as self-loathing. As I was to learn from Debbie, self-loathing, as well as other unprocessed emotions from these experiences, physically manifested in my body as cancer.

I entered the hospital at the end of July 2008 for another experimental treatment, which included a bone-marrow transplant. The treatment regimen itself was so harsh that they thought it might kill me, and thus stated that my chances of even surviving the treatment and leaving the hospital were 1 in 3. I was told to gain 30 pounds prior to the hospitalization, as I would be very ill after the transplant. Between the vomiting and diarrhea, doctors said I would probably lose *at least* 30 pounds.

For ten days before the transplant, I was filled with massive doses of chemotherapy. Debbie instructed me to use the Infinite Love & Gratitude hand sign to harmonize all of the chemotherapy, as well as any IV fluids or medications that went into my body. The hospital gave me cases of bottled water to drink, and per

Debbie's guidance, I wrote "Infinite Love & Gratitude" on each and every one I drank. As for the horrible reaction I was supposed to have after the transplant, I vomited twice and lost a total of three pounds. Meanwhile, 6 of the 12 people on the unit undergoing the same procedure died while I was there, and another was given "end of life" care.

I did have one challenge while I was in the hospital. I developed a yeast infection in my lungs and had to undergo surgery. But ten weeks after I entered, I left the hospital feeling better than I had felt in 20 years!

I go in for monthly checkups and have been declared cancer free since November 2008. The doctors are astounded—surprised I am even alive, and they have absolutely no explanation. They call it a miracle. What I know is that The LifeLine Technique works. Truthfully, I had my doubts in the beginning, but do not doubt it anymore. I am eternally grateful for Debbie and this technique with every breath I take.[3]

The Energy Pathways of the Body

The roots of muscle-reflex testing (MRT) date back to the ancient practice of traditional Chinese medicine. More than 5,000 years ago, there was documented evidence of a system of energy pathways throughout the body, commonly referred to as *acupuncture meridians.* Acupuncturists knew that placing needles in specific points along the meridian to decrease or increase the flow of energy (also known as *chi*) would impact all areas of the body and its harmonious connection with nature.

It took a few more centuries for the Western world to understand the links between these energy pathways and the physical body. The science that emerged midway through the 20th century was *kinesiology,* a broad term that refers to the study of the biomechanical movement of the body. Kinesiology was pioneered in the 1940s by a pair of physiotherapists, Henry and Florence Kendall, who developed a method to ascertain the strength of a muscle. Their work is the basis for modern-day physical therapy.[4]

63

Thirty years later, the late George Goodheart, D.C., developed *Applied Kinesiology* (AK), which built upon the Kendalls' work and was incorporated into chiropractic techniques. Initially, the most striking finding of Dr. Goodheart was a clear demonstration that muscles instantly became weak when the body was exposed to harmful stimuli and instantly strong when exposed to substances that were therapeutic. Dr. Goodheart built a solid, scientifically based system of research and teaching that ultimately led to the formation of the International College of Applied Kinesiology (ICAK).

The late John Thie, D.C., one of the original members of Dr. Goodheart's AK team, simplified the work. Dr. Thie introduced a series of challenges or tests that enabled the system of muscle testing to be used as an assessment of imbalances by both professionals and laypeople. This system is known as Touch for Health (TFH). Alan Beardall, D.C., added "hand modes" to the process of muscle testing, after discovering that the muscle response differed depending upon the position of his hands when he touched a specific point. His work is called *Clinical Kinesiology* (CK). John Diamond, a psychiatrist, also began using kinesiology in the treatment of psychiatric patients, an application he labeled "behavioral kinesiology." Over the years, Dr. Goodheart's findings became the foundation for many more techniques, including Total Body Modification (TBM), Neuro Emotional Technique (NET), and Applied Psycho-Neurobiology (APN).

Does muscle-reflex testing work? David Hawkins—a world-renowned scientist, researcher, and medical doctor—publicly conducted MRT experiments. While lecturing to audiences of 1,000 people, he distributed 500 unmarked envelopes containing artificial sweetener and 500 identical envelopes containing vitamin C.[5] Of the experience, he wrote:

> The audience would then be divided up and would alternate testing each other. When the envelopes were opened, the audience reaction was always one of amazement and delight when they saw that everybody had gone weak in response to the artificial sweetener and strong in response to the vitamin C.[6]

Just like the autonomic nervous system, MRT is a polarity-dependent mechanism. The muscle "locks out" or maintains its strength as long as there's a congruency with the function, adaptability, and survival of the entire organism.[7] When there is *incongruence,* meaning imbalance, an indicator muscle will give way rather than lock out. During a session with The LifeLine Technique, rather than asking yes-or-no questions, MRT is being used to assess the source of the *balance* or *imbalance* manifesting as a physical symptom or stress.

Let's practice muscle-reflex testing. This is the first tool in your arsenal for interpreting the secret code of your mind.

⊕⊕⊕ ⊕⊕⊕

CHAPTER 10

Guidelines for
Muscle-Reflex Testing

*"Muscle Reflex Testing . . . provides access to powerful techniques
for effecting change and reinforcing that change in the whole person,
physically, mentally, emotionally, and spiritually."*

— John Thie, D.C.

Getting to know someone often takes concerted effort and time; the process can feel awkward. By teaching you how to use muscle-reflex testing (MRT), I'm offering you an opportunity to establish a new and authentic relationship with your *whole* self— a relationship that opens the door to learning who you *really* are so that you can awaken to the infinite potential you possess to be your true self.

Mastering the art of MRT is like learning to ride a bicycle for the first time—it takes practice. The goal is to experience the change in the muscle reflex . . . it's an obvious reaction when the muscle "locks out" or "gives way." The first time you experience the MRT as it "gives way" may be surprising because your conscious mind has one intention and your subconscious mind overrides it. However, once you're able to differentiate between the "lock out" and the "give way," you've got it forever.

Because MRT is one of the cornerstones of The LifeLine Technique, learning how to do it and being comfortable with the process is essential. The following guidelines for self-testing, accompanied by photos, demonstrate MRT. Simply do your best to follow the instructions. It is important, for instance, to say aloud "Hold strong" in order to engage your *conscious* mind in the MRT process.

First and foremost, be patient and loving with yourself. Have fun!

Guidelines for Using MRT to Self-Test

MRT indicator muscle.   MRT "gives way."

1. Bend your arm (whichever feels most comfortable) at the elbow to create a 90-degree angle, as pictured.

2. Place your other hand on the bent arm just above the wrist, as pictured.

3. Have a clear intention and use Present Time Consciousness to focus on MRT.

4. To feel a mild resistance, imagine that you're holding a one-liter bottle of water in the hand of your bent arm while you're performing MRT.

5. Say aloud, "Hold strong." Using your free hand, slowly and confidently press down on your bent arm in order to feel the conscious "lock out" of a muscle reflex. This is what we call the "zero-point."

6. Remember that the subconscious muscle reflex will always override a conscious choice.

7. Remember that you are *feeling* for a change in the muscle reflex.

The next section contains an exercise that will allow you to feel the difference between the "lock out" and "give way" of muscle-reflex testing.

Muscle-Reflex-Testing Exercise

As noted earlier in the book, in the late 1990s, Masaru Emoto's research was the first to provide pictures that reveal how water reflects the consciousness of its environment. Because your body is composed of two-thirds water, the quality of your life is intimately connected to the structure of that water.[1] When your cells are exposed to the vibration of "love" versus "hate," there's an immediate reaction or reflection in the structure of the water that composes them, and therefore in the function of the cells themselves. Let's look at these pictures once again to appreciate the impact that words have on the structural integrity of water:

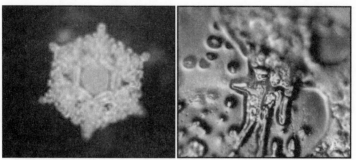

Love & Gratitude.   I Hate You—I'll Kill You.

With the first MRT practice exercise, you'll test Dr. Emoto's research yourself by using the words *love* and *hate*. Do your best to observe from your heart rather than from your head whether you *feel* the reflex "give way" or "lock out" during the exercise. Let your body's intelligence guide you.

"Love" and "Hate" Muscle-Reflex Test

1. Using the MRT indicator muscle, begin with the "zero-point" by saying aloud, "Hold strong." Confidently and gently press on the bent arm. You will feel the "lock out."

2. Say aloud: "Love, love, love, hold strong."

3. Now confidently yet gently press down on your bent arm, feeling for the reflex response. You will still feel the "lock out" of the reflex.

4. Now, say aloud: "Hate, hate, hate, hold strong."

5. Next, confidently yet gently press down on your arm, feeling for the reflex response. You will feel the MRT indicator muscle "give way."

6. Now, again say aloud: "Love, love, love, hold strong." Recheck the MRT indicator muscle; you'll feel the "lock out" of the MRT again.

Did you feel it? It's an amazing awakening when you do! Practice this exercise again and again until you begin to become confident about feeling the "lock out" or the "give way" in the MRT indicator muscle. By practicing, you're creating a new neural network and muscle memory, helping you become sensitive to subtle reactive changes. Have fun playing!

As we learned from Dr. Emoto, water exposed to love forms a beautiful, crystalline structure. Water exposed to hate immediately *loses* its crystalline nature. Physicists have found that the more crystalline a structure is, the greater its electromagnetic conductance. The reverse is also true—a less crystalline structure results in a decrease in conductance. Considering that your nervous system (brain and reflexes) communicates with every cell in your body via electromagnetic synapses conducted by the water in your cells, every one of your thoughts, feelings, and actions will have a direct impact on your ability to maintain balance and inner peace, and ultimately to achieve optimal health.

Can You Use MRT with Animals?

In 2008, my wife, Sarit, noticed that our cat Zen was excessively licking the area around his anus. I personally wasn't bothered by it . . . that's what cats do. However, when I turned Zen over, there was a three-inch ulcerated wound. I immediately used myself as a surrogate and began conducting a session on him using The LifeLine Technique. As it turns out, Zen just needed the simple 1-2-3 PLAN that you're learning in this book! Three days later the wound was completely healed.

Ready for the Next Step?

Now that you've learned the basics of how to conduct a muscle-reflex test, what do you do with it? In the next chapter, you'll discover your most powerful tool for creating inner peace—the Infinite Love & Gratitude Sequence (ILS).

⊕⊕⊕ ⊕⊕⊕

CHAPTER 11

The Infinite Love & Gratitude Sequence (ILS)

"When you experience love in any form . . . you are healing your body. Love takes you out of a state of resistance. . . ."

— Eva M. Selhub, M.D.

I'm often in awe of the simplicity of The LifeLine Technique and its basic premise—that love is the bridge between the subconscious and conscious minds, and that it's the catalyst for healing and transformation, resulting in inner peace. Another pioneer in the field of mind-body healing, Leonard Laskow, M.D., describes it in this way: "Love is the energy of *between* that opens to *beyond*."[1]

When I refer to the simplicity of The LifeLine Technique, I'm talking about the Infinite Love & Gratitude Sequence (ILS) used to harmonize and transform symptoms and stress. Other modalities of healing or treatment use a therapeutic model based upon something or someone being wrong, broken, or dysfunctional. However, The LifeLine Technique's philosophy is deeply rooted in the knowledge and understanding of life's divine perfection. It recognizes and incorporates the genius of nature . . . the profound power of allowing rather than resisting, accepting rather than judging, and loving rather than fearing.

When your body or life is speaking with symptoms and stress, as noted earlier, it means there's a subconscious emotion that's ready to be processed. The ILS is a *universal* healing frequency. It uses the power of Infinite Love & Gratitude, along with the mudra for "I love you" common in American Sign Language.

Dr. Emoto has written that the harmony of love and gratitude is the "greatest form of energy."[2] And in *Power vs. Force*, Dr. Hawkins writes about the potency of hand mudras as a catalyst for enlightenment "wherein the palm of the hand radiates benediction [i.e., love]—this is the act of transmitting this energy field to the consciousness of mankind."[3]

Take a moment and make the "I love you" mudra, as pictured.

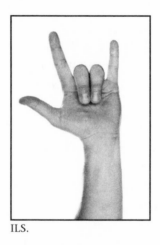

ILS.

To make that sign, fully expand your thumb and all fingers away from each other. Fold down your middle and ring fingers while keeping your thumb, index finger, and pinky fully extended. Place the "I love you" mudra over your heart. Say aloud, "Infinite Love & Gratitude."

What do you feel? Some people say they feel warmth radiating throughout their bodies; others report feeling calm and peaceful.

Can the ILS alone make a difference? Whenever I experience any type of stress in my mind or body, the very first action I take (and I've taught my children to do the same) is to place the "I love you" mudra over my heart and say aloud, "Infinite Love & Gratitude."

The following instructions combine the use of the Infinite Love & Gratitude Sequence (ILS) and muscle-reflex testing (MRT), which you learned in the last chapter.

MRT indicator muscle.   MRT "gives way."   ILS next to body.

1. Using the bent-arm indicator muscle to conduct muscle-reflex testing (MRT), say aloud, "Hold strong" to feel the "lock out," also known as "zero-point."

2. Now, think about a stressful situation in your life.

3. Once you're tuned in to the stressful experience, say aloud again: "Hold strong." You will feel the MRT indicator muscle immediately "give way."

4. Now hold your hand in the ILS hand position while saying aloud: "Infinite Love & Gratitude." Allow yourself to truly *feel* the Infinite Love & Gratitude.

5. Now, go back and think about the stressful situation. Recheck the MRT indicator muscle by saying, "Hold strong." You

will feel the MRT indicator muscle "lock out" while connecting to the stressful situation.

6. If you don't feel the "lock out," repeat Steps 4 and 5 until the MRT "locks out."

You may notice that the stressful situation has shifted—that it's more difficult to connect to it. This is what I call "LifeLine Technique First Aid." It helps you reconnect to Infinite Love & Gratitude in the midst of a stressful situation so that you can move through it.

Awakening to Your Potential for Peace

The ILS is done with intention in order to create an attractor field—a life force of feeling. Seeing someone perform the ILS will provide you with clarity and show you its simplicity.

Learning how to use MRT and the ILS is both fun and exciting. Take your time and practice often. Remember, experience is the greatest teacher. Begin a study group with the intention of practicing and mastering this art and science of the mind.

If you can drive a car, sing the alphabet song, write a sentence, or perform anything that is simultaneously creative and logical, you'll be able to learn these skills. Anything worth learning and doing requires vision, discipline, and the passion to do your best. Go for it!

⊕⊕⊕ ⊕⊕⊕

CHAPTER 12

The LifeLine Technique
Flow Chart: In Search of
Life's Greatest Treasures

*"Confusion is an opportunity to rearrange an experience and organize
it in a different way than you normally would. That allows you to
learn something new and to see and hear the world in a new way."*

— Richard Bandler

With the advent of GPS as standard equipment in cars and cell
phones, or step-by-step routes available for download online, paper
maps are almost obsolete. Although the format and accessibility
of information has changed, the need still remains—when you're
searching for the right direction, which way do you go?

I believe that your search to find the right direction and answers
to your questions about your life—in the face of high levels of
stress or anxiety, aging parents or young children, financial crises,
or your own chronic health challenges—led you to this book. You
are now holding in your hands the treasure map that will lead you
to the pathway for inner peace.

The LifeLine Technique Flow Chart has 16 steps—each one
of which provides the foundation for the next. You're about to
embark on a journey, an adventure. And the treasure that you'll
find upon your arrival is priceless.

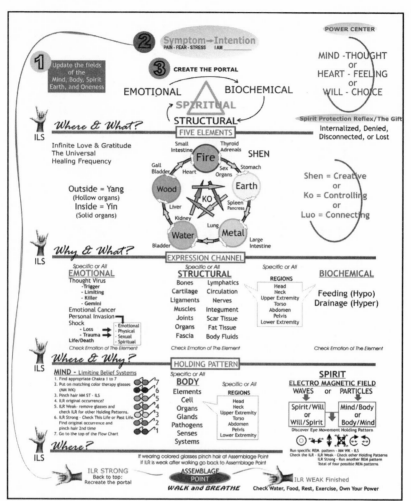

The most recent version of The LifeLine Technique Flow Chart.

The LifeLine Technique Flow Chart is your invitation to not only believe in your dreams, but to live them. I am offering you the opportunity for optimal health, mutually respectful and loving relationships, and unbridled appreciation and passion just for being alive. Take action now and step out of the worldview that "peace is impossible." Within all conflict resides the unborn wisdom of love and the power to shine. These are the 16 steps:

Step 1:   The Reconnection
Step 2:   Symptom-Stress → Intention
Step 3:   Create the Portal
Step 4:   The Triad
Step 5:   The Power Center
Step 6:   Spirit Protection Reflex (SPR)/the Gift
Step 7:   The Five Elements and Their Metaphors
Step 8:   Specific Meridians
Step 9:   Cycle of the Emotion
Step 10:   Expression Channel
Step 11:   Check Emotions
Step 12:   Holding Pattern
Step 13:   Assemblage Point
Step 14:   The Challenge—Walk and Breathe
Step 15:   The ILR
Step 16:   The Five Basics for Optimal Health

The 1-2-3 PLAN

Let's begin to navigate your journey to inner peace. The first 3 of the 16 steps of The LifeLine Technique Flow Chart are called "The 1-2-3 PLAN," and are numbered at the top of the chart. *PLAN* stands for Preliminary LifeLine Assessment Navigator, and it details the three easy steps to navigate and transform pain into power, fear into courage, and stress into inspiration. Learning the 1-2-3 PLAN will awaken you to living a life that is both meaningful and exciting.

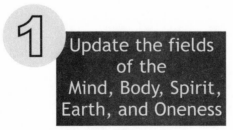

Step 1: The Reconnection.

79

Step 2: Symptom-Stress → Intention.

Step 3: Create the Portal.

The 1-2-3 PLAN is like a navigational system used by a sea captain—it guides you in setting the appropriate course for bridging the gap between the conscious and subconscious minds. The purpose of this section of the book is to help you understand the true meaning of symptoms and stress and to provide the specific steps of transformation through the power of your mind.

⊕⊕⊕ ⊕⊕⊕

CHAPTER 13

Step 1: The Reconnection—Expanding Your Sense of Oneness

"The energy of the mind is the essence of life."
— Aristotle

The belief that we are all engaged in an intimate and interdependent relationship with all life in the universe is part of the philosophy of nearly all indigenous cultures around the world. This web of oneness has been broadly termed the *Field*. Journalist Lynne McTaggart's book *The Field* provides an all-encompassing definition:

> The field is the force, rather than germs or genes, that finally determines whether we are healthy or ill, the force which must be tapped in order to heal. We are attached and engaged, indivisible from our world, and our only fundamental truth is our relationship with it. "The field," as Einstein once succinctly put it, "is the only reality."[1]

Scientists involved in the area of quantum physics have demonstrated that the Field is interactive; our thoughts, feelings, and beliefs impact what's going on around us, as well as what

81

happens outside.[2] In other words, through our interaction with the Field, we're both the directors and actors of our reality.

When your mind, body, and spirit are disconnected, it means that a part of you is disconnected from the Field. As a result, your ability to shine and thrive in the moment is limited by the level of your connection.

It's easy to look at something "outside of you" as being separate from yourself. However, this perception inhibits you from realizing your highest potential and power. The truth is that everything and everyone is interconnected. The nature of your mind, body, and spirit is holographic—simultaneously multidimensional.

Because your body and life are microcosms of the universal macrocosm, this same principle applies to the planet. There's a subtle web binding everything and everyone—a web of emotion[3]—the purpose of which is to keep things moving, changing, and evolving. It may appear that the objects in your body or life are static, solid, and separate, but there's an intimate and intricate quantum order at the heart of it all. With The LifeLine Technique sessions, you're able to quickly and simply distill and transform symptoms and stress. As a result, you awaken to a whole new level of awareness, abilities, and choices.

Nature Is the Field

My friend Carol Freeman is a professional nature photographer whose Zen-like eye for detail captures breathtaking and awe-inspiring images. In 2003, Carol began The Endangered Species Photography Project.[4] It's a work in progress, yet she's well under way in her efforts to photograph the nearly 500 threatened or endangered species in the state of Illinois. Her intention is to raise awareness about the environment through the compelling imagery she catalogs.

I refer to Carol as the "Nature Whisperer." Simply by observing her emotive photographs of flowers, insects, birds, animals, trees, and lakes, you're instilled with a deep connection with nature and a profound sense of oneness. Nature is the physical personification of the Field—that place where we are, as Lynne McTaggart put it, "attached and engaged."

Step 1: The Reconnection

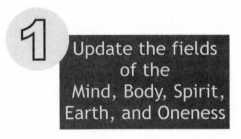

You can follow these steps either seated or standing—the most important thing is to be comfortable. With Step 1, you'll reconnect to Present Time Consciousness (PTC).

Here are pictures of the specific hand positions for the different connections:

Close-up of crown fingers.

Spirit connection.

Mind connection.

Body connection.

Earth connection.

Oneness connection.

84

Spirit-Body Connection

Harmonizing the connection between
the spirit and the body.

1. Touch all of your fingers together, as pictured, and place these five touching fingers on top of the crown-chakra connection point of the head, which is referred to in traditional Chinese medicine as the *Du-20/Bahui acupuncture point.* In Chinese, *Bahui* is defined as the "point of hundred meeting places," and it is said to be the location through which the spirit enters and leaves the body at the moment of conception, during sleep, in times of stress, and at the moment of death.

2. Place the index finger of your other hand on the body connection point, in the midline of the chest over the heart chakra, where the thymus gland is located. (See photo.)

3. With your fingers in their respective positions, say aloud, "Infinite Love & Gratitude to harmonizing my spirit to my body."

Harmonize the connection between the body and spirit.

4. Remove the five fingers from the spirit connection point on top of your head and immediately return them to the same place while maintaining the body connection point.

5. With your fingers in their respective positions, say aloud, "Infinite Love & Gratitude to harmonizing my body to my spirit."

The spirit and body are in harmony.

6. Simultaneously remove the five fingers from the spirit connection point on top of your head and the finger on the body connection point, and return them simultaneously.

7. With your fingers returned to their respective positions, say aloud, "Infinite Love & Gratitude to my spirit and body being unified and harmonized as one."

Mind-Body Connection

Harmonize the connection between the mind and the body.

1. First place your flat hand on your forehead, as pictured. This is the mind connection point. Now put a finger on the body connection point.

2. With your hand on your forehead and your finger on the body connection point, say aloud, "Infinite Love & Gratitude to harmonizing my mind to my body."

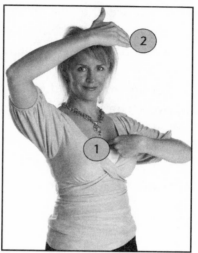

Harmonize the connection between the body and the mind.

3. Now lift the mind connection point away from your forehead and place it back down again over the same place on your forehead while you continue to touch the body connection point.

4. While maintaining this position, say aloud, "Infinite Love & Gratitude to harmonizing my body to my mind."

The mind and body in harmony.

5. Remove your flat hand from the mind connection point and your index finger from the body connection point simultaneously, and then return them at the same time. While maintaining this position, say aloud, "Infinite Love & Gratitude to my mind and body being unified and harmonized as one."

Earth Connection

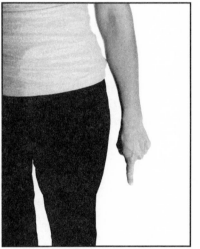

Earth Connection.

1. Point to the ground, focusing your intention on the core thriving nature of Mother Earth. Use your other hand to place a finger on the body connection point.

Harmonize the Earth connection to the body.

Harmonize the Earth connection to the mind.

Harmonize the Earth connection to the spirit.

2. Say aloud, "Infinite Love & Gratitude to harmonizing the thriving nature of Mother Earth to my body."

3. Keep pointing to the Earth while placing your flat hand over the mind connection point.

4. Say aloud, "Infinite Love & Gratitude to harmonizing the thriving nature of Mother Earth to my mind."

5. Continue pointing to the earth while placing all of your fingers, touching together, to your spirit connection point.

6. Say aloud, "Infinite Love & Gratitude to harmonizing the thriving nature of Mother Earth to my spirit."

Universal Field of Oneness Connection

Connection to Oneness.

1. Place your hands in the prayer position in front of the heart chakra with the intention of connecting to your higher purpose, Source, or the Universal Field of Oneness.

Harmonize the Universal Field of Oneness connection to the body.

Harmonize the Universal Field of Oneness connection to the mind.

Harmonize the Universal Field of Oneness connection to the spirit.

91

2. As pictured, move your hands in prayer position to the body connection point and say aloud, "Infinite Love & Gratitude to harmonizing the Universal Field of Oneness to my body."

3. Keeping your hands in the prayer position, now place them in front of the mind connection point and say aloud, "Infinite Love & Gratitude to harmonizing the Universal Field of Oneness to my mind."

4. With your hands still in the same position, now place them on the spirit connection point and say aloud, "Infinite Love & Gratitude to harmonizing the Universal Field of Oneness to my spirit."

5. Go to *Step 2: Symptom-Stress → Intention.*

A Wonderful Daily Practice

Harmonizing your connections to the body, mind, spirit, earth, and Universal Field of Oneness is a wonderful daily practice. The optimal time to do so is five minutes before going to bed and right as you become conscious of your breath when you wake up in the morning. These are the times you're closest to being in a complete subconscious state yet still able to make a conscious choice. During sleep, the subconscious mind downloads information from the experiences of your day and integrates those experiences into long-term memory.

In addition, if you find yourself in a stressful situation during the day with no opportunity to run the entire 1-2-3 PLAN, *Step 1: The Reconnection* followed by walking in place while breathing deeply, along with using the ILS (giving yourself Infinite Love & Gratitude), will help you reconnect to Present Time Consciousness. You'll tune in to what you're feeling and move through it with grace and ease on the way to unleashing your greatest potential and power.

⊕⊕⊕

The Reconnection is just the beginning! The next step on the road to inner peace is *Step 2: Symptom-Stress → Intention.* In the following chapter, you'll learn how to identify symptoms and stress and set your intention for healing and wholeness. Out of all the 16 steps of The LifeLine Technique Flow Chart, I've discovered that Step 2 unleashes the most profound alchemy for helping you consciously appreciate the significant role the subconscious mind plays in your life. Step 2 activates the law of attraction on a subconscious level.

⊕⊕⊕ ⊕⊕⊕

CHAPTER 14

Step 2: Creating
What Is Possible, Now!

*"Think of NOW as a bridge. One side of the bridge is our past
comprised of all events, probabilities, and choices that have led us
to our NOW. On the other side of the bridge is our future, containing
all the possible and probable realities. The bridge, or our NOW,
is our point of control and power through our intentions."*

— Adam, intuitive healer

According to The LifeLine Law of Transformation and Creation,
*emotions transform energy; energy creates movement; movement is
change; and change is the essence of life.*[1] But what happens to your
body and relationships when your emotions *(energy in motion)*
are somehow stifled? What does your body and life do with *that*
energy? From the outset of my career in holistic healing, my quest
has been to answer those questions, and more: *Why* does the body
break down? Why is life stressful for one person and inspirational
for another?

My early training in chiropractic taught me that symptoms
were the result of an impingement on the nervous system. More
often than not, however, after adjusting the spine and balancing
the nervous system, I found that the symptom would return.

Chinese medicine and acupuncture taught me that symptoms were connected to a deficiency or excess of *chi* (energy or life force) flowing through the meridians. Combining chiropractic and acupuncture resulted in amazing healing results; nevertheless, symptoms continued to recur or linger.

Later, when I learned other healing modalities such as Applied Kinesiology (AK) and Total Body Modification (TBM), I grew to understand the meaning of *functional physiology,* which represents the dynamic state of communication that is always occurring between cells, organs, glands, and systems of the body. This dialogue occurs subconsciously on both an individual and a collective level at the same time. The intention of a functional physiological process is the striving toward balance while maintaining imbalance. The physical ebb-and-flow movement is the body's evolutionary journey of spiritual transformation.

Using reflex points on the body, skull, or spine, these systems of functional physiology taught me how to activate the function of blood-sugar metabolism, neurological processes, digestion, detoxification, blood pressure, hormonal balance, and the immune system. My clients have appreciated the eclectic combination of modalities I've been trained in as a result of my passion and thirst for knowledge. For me, however, there continued to be something missing. My search for a seamless system that merged *everything* I knew continued to elude me until I awakened to The LifeLine Technique.

What makes this technique unique is its revolutionary way of understanding the dialogue of symptoms and stress. With it, that language can be decoded, interpreted, harmonized, and transformed with Infinite Love & Gratitude, balancing the *root* causes of all pain, fear, and stress.

Transforming the Symptoms of Fibromyalgia

For 26 years, Ava suffered from a wide array of symptoms, including depression, chronic pain, insomnia, and fatigue.

After she had gone to several doctors for more than 20 years in search of relief from the symptoms, one doctor finally gave her a diagnosis—*fibromyalgia*—which he told her was the result of post-Lyme syndrome. The doctor gave Ava a prescription for pain medication; and he recommended she consider taking antidepressants to deal with the depression, insomnia, and fatigue she'd also been experiencing. Ava decided that she didn't want to take the antidepressants and continued to consult more medical doctors. Each of these physicians told her they couldn't help her since she declined to follow their recommended drug protocol. Ava decided to seek out alternative-health practitioners because she realized that the allopathic community knew very little about fibromyalgia.

Ava's transformational journey with The LifeLine Technique began in 2008, and she saw me for about one year. The subconscious emotional response patterns were associated with an inability to speak her truth, resulting in toxic levels of internalized and denied anger and rage.

All symptoms manifesting as autoimmune imbalances—such as fibromyalgia, multiple sclerosis, and lupus—do have one thing in common: on a subconscious level, the client is disconnected from self-love. As a consequence, the body attacks itself. However, even though the root of the symptom is similar, the journey to heal from this diagnosis is specific for each and every person.

After one of her last sessions, Ava sent me the following e-mail:

> A week or two after my first session, I was amazed to realize that I hadn't in fact experienced any of the chronic pain that is constant with fibromyalgia, and that I had taken no medication or other pain relievers whatsoever!
>
> I've used many, many different healing methodologies over the years, and I can honestly say that nothing has alleviated the pain from fibromyalgia even remotely as well as The LifeLine Technique. Your unwavering dedication to both your vision and to The LifeLine Technique itself is quite a breakthrough—a great

blessing, which I suspect, in time, will inevitably turn much of the conventional science of medicine and pharmacology on its head.

The technique brings with it the potential to redefine the meaning of health and healing on a global scale. Thank you, Dr. Darren, for having fortitude and determination in making all of this so, *and* for helping me find the answers to healing I've been seeking.[2]

Tuning In to the Subtle Dialogue

Most people are so disconnected from their bodies that sometimes observing feelings or pain can be a challenging process. Think of the person who says, "I have a high pain threshold." The truth is, they're disconnected!

Take a moment right now and observe how your body is "speaking" to you. As you tune in to its subtle dialogue, take your time and write down all your findings in your journal. The more you practice scanning your body and writing down your feelings, the better you'll become at "hearing" when it's "speaking" to you.

Are you aware of any physical symptoms? Maybe you're feeling frustrated and helpless, or anxious and afraid as a result of them? Regardless of how or what you're feeling, these are your *feelings*. They're nothing *more* than feelings. Their purpose is to get your attention. They're not here to victimize you or cause suffering. That would be a complete misunderstanding of the language stemming from your subconscious mind. Physical symptoms are a spiritual feedback mechanism activated to awaken you to the power of living your life intentionally.

The same holds true with the stressors of life. Stressful and upsetting relationships or experiences stem from the subconscious mind. Take a moment to observe what or *who* is causing you to feel stressed or upset. As you do so, write down in your journal whatever or whomever comes to mind.

More than a journaling exercise about what's bothering you, focusing on the stress—or how your body is "speaking" to you—sets the stage for you to use The LifeLine Technique to discover the *root cause* of that expression of stress. Remember that this experience is *only* stressful or painful because you're not consciously aware of the contents of the message from the subconscious mind.

The healing process begins when you *consciously awaken and live from the perspective* that the symptom is an invitation to dialogue rather than the launch of an assault. When you observe symptoms in this manner, you enter a state of appreciation and gratitude where the meaning and value of all experiences are revealed.

Your goal now is to consciously choose your new response, which I refer to as *setting the intention.* The intention becomes the catalyst for discovery. You'll understand why when you read the next section.

Setting the Intention

Have you ever driven your car; boarded an airplane, bus, or train; or ridden the subway without having a particular destination in mind? With the exception of vacations or the occasional need to "get lost," the answer is generally no. When you're going somewhere, it's important to have a clear intention. The same is true with the healing process, as explained by Deepak Chopra, M.D., in *Perfect Health:*

> The first secret you should know about perfect health is that you have to choose it. You can only be as healthy as you think it is possible to be. . . . It involves a total shift in perspective that makes disease and infirm old age unacceptable.[3]

To achieve optimal or "perfect" health, setting a clear intention is essential, and that's why this is Step 2 of The LifeLine Technique Flow Chart.

Setting an intention is more than a positive affirmation, however. In quantum physics, there's a concept known as the "observer effect," which is explained exceptionally well in layperson's terms in Gregg Braden's books *The Divine Matrix* and

The Spontaneous Healing of Belief. The "observer effect" tells us that our very observation of an event changes the outcome.[4]

Fred Wolf, Ph.D., who is best known as "Dr. Quantum" in the film *What the Bleep Do We Know!?,* further defines this observation as any action that causes a choice to be made, which consequently impacts both the conscious and subconscious minds.[5] When you set an intention, you're making a conscious choice, setting up the conditions for the "observer effect" to take hold and creating the conditions for your subconscious mind to help manifest the reality that your conscious mind is seeking to create. An intention activates neurons in the brain by actually sending signals from one to another; the intention gives directions to specific healing pathways.[6]

There have been numerous studies on how intention impacts the physiology of the body. Biofeedback has shown that the mind can be used to control many bodily functions such as skin temperature, pain, and the healing of tissues.[7] In the book *The Intention Experiment,* journalist Lynne McTaggart reports on a study by the Institute for Research on Unlimited Love at Case Western Reserve University, based in Cleveland, Ohio. The study found that when an intention is sent, every major physiological system is mirrored in the body of the receiver. Their conclusion: "Intention is the perfect manifestation of love."[8]

See Yourself in Control of Your Destiny

When you're creating your intention, be sure to activate all of your senses, fully experiencing your intention as if the goal has *already* been achieved. See and feel yourself, for example, being in control of your destiny. According to medical doctor and author Leonard Laskow, when you set an intention, it's important to understand the difference between "what you want to accomplish by your words, actions, reactions, goals, achievements, and beliefs, and the positive intent behind it all—which is what is *really* wanted . . . freedom, love, peace, empowerment, happiness, or understanding."[9]

With *Step 2: Symptom-Stress → Intention* of The LifeLine Technique Flow Chart, you become an alchemist. You use positive intentions to convert symptoms and stress into opportunities to unleash infinite possibilities for healing and wholeness.

One of life's more perplexing and sometimes frustrating challenges is that you don't get to choose what happens to you. The beauty, however, is that you *do* have a choice about how you respond to any and all situations. Your conscious mind allows you to change anything, regardless of circumstances. The ficus tree in my office, on the other hand, lacks a conscious mind. Consequently, it merely reacts by growing toward the sun. It relies upon me to turn it every once in a while so that it will grow evenly. The ability to choose is what separates human beings from all other species on the planet.

The symptoms or stress being expressed by your body and life are something that you'd never *consciously* choose. They stem from the subconscious mind and are reactive in nature. Once you're able to recognize the significant difference between a conscious choice and a subconscious reaction, it will be a profound realization that will forever change your life.

Step 2: Symptom-Stress → Intention

With this step, you're connecting to your conscious awareness about the symptoms and stress speaking through your body and life. You'll then set an intention based upon where you're going rather than the symptoms and stress you'd like to get rid of or have go away. For your intention, you can review the list that you made in the Introduction of the book or create new ones to manifest a transformation in your body and life today.

1. In your journal, write out whatever physical symptoms you're experiencing. Take a moment right now and simply observe your body. Rather than being identified, defined, or diagnosed by the symptoms in your body, remember to bring your awareness to them in order to discover their authentic meaning and value.

What's catching your attention? Are you aware of any pain, tightness, itching, or numbness? What's the quality of this feeling: Is it sharp or dull, localized or diffuse? On a scale of 0 to 10, where 0 is no feeling at all and 10 is the most extreme it could possibly be, what do you rate this physical feeling? What emotion do you feel, knowing that your body is physically speaking to you in this way?

Take your time and write these answers down. The location of these physical symptoms is what you'll use to create a Conscious Body Portal.

2. Now tune in to your life and take a moment to observe what or who in it is causing you to feel stressed or upset. Ask yourself, "What has happened, or hasn't happened, that's causing me to feel this way?" What emotion do you feel as you're now connecting to that person or experience? What do you rate that emotion on a scale of 0 to 10?

In your journal, write down the name of the person or experience creating the stress, the emotion you're feeling associated with the stress, and the number you rate it.

3. Now ask yourself, "Would I ever wake up and consciously *choose* to create my day filled with these physical symptoms or stressful experiences?" The answer will always be *Never!*

4. Knowing that you'd never *consciously choose* these symptoms or stressors but are still experiencing them helps you recognize the truth of their origin . . . an emotional reaction stemming from your subconscious mind. Instead of living a subconscious life of reacting to reactions, you're now going to consciously lead your subconscious mind to where you want to be, both physically and emotionally.

Set your intention as if you were already there. If you were already where you wanted to be, you'd be in the Divine land of "I am," which means that you're in the present moment. When you set an intention of where you want to be as if you're already there, your subconscious mind has no choice—it begins the process of reacting from this place. Also, your brain and body aren't designed to be able to tell the difference between memory, the present moment, and imagination; and as a result, your body and life begin the process of reacting from this future place.

Now, use your imagination from your heart's desire and the purpose of your soul to set your intention: "I am _____." An example is: "I am filled with joy and laughter." Write your "I am" intention in your journal.

5. Imagine yourself living a life with your "I am" intention. How might doing so impact the health of your body or the relationships in your life? How do you feel emotionally envisioning your thoughts, feelings, words, and actions stemming from this "I am" intention? An example may be: "I feel confident!" Write down this feeling next to your "I am" intention. Remember, you need to feel if you want to heal.

This *feeling* from the "I am _____" intention will begin your journey of *Step 3: Create the Portal* to your subconscious mind. The Conscious Mind Present-Past-Future Declarative Statements Portal will now open the door to your infinite subconscious mind. We're building a bridge of consciousness. Remember that a bridge allows two sides to meet that would otherwise never connect.

Armed with an understanding of symptoms and stress, and having a clear vision about your intention, you're now ready to learn about *Step 3: Create the Portal*. Think of Step 3 as a crossroads—the crossroads to inner peace.

⊕⊕⊕ ⊕⊕⊕

CHAPTER 15

Step 3: Opening the Doorway to Your Authentic Self

*". . . an indigenous wise man, a Hopi Elder, tells us that
'We are the Ones we have been waiting for.' We . . .
are the only ones who can turn disaster into opportunity;
we are the ones who can understand our interconnectedness in
the great web of life and our power to honor it, treat it as sacred,
cease damaging it, restore it. Will we understand that in time?"*

— Elisabet Sahtouris, Ph.D.

When your body or life feels out of sync . . . when you're in pain, experiencing fear, or living with stress and anxiety . . . there's a gap. This gap between your conscious and subconscious minds represents a protective mechanism—a subconscious emotional pattern of reaction. It consists of limiting beliefs, unprocessed memories, traumas, or other experiences that you were unable to consciously integrate. The chasm between the conscious and subconscious minds represents *your* unborn potential. That potential can only be activated when the gap is bridged. It's the failure to tap into that unborn potential that's inhibiting you from knowing and *being* your authentic self; it's the gap that prevents you from achieving your dreams or living a passionate, joyful, and peace-filled life.

The subconscious mind is precise in its ability to react in each and every moment. It doesn't think—it's mechanistic. Like a light switch that turns on or off, creating a light or dark environment, the reactions triggered within the subconscious mind are either based upon love (light) or fear (dark). It's that simple, but not always so easy to recognize and accept as a gift. That's why I refer to symptoms and stress as "gifts in strange wrapping paper." When you're in the throes of dark or fearful thoughts, feelings, and actions, it's hard to imagine the world beyond that shroud of pain and suffering. However, everything happens for a reason. With The LifeLine Technique, you *use* the darkness to find the light; you journey beneath the surface and translate the conversation with your subconscious mind to find the meaning and value of every experience. When you shift your consciousness to recognize that every symptom or stressful experience has a subconscious root, you unleash the potential to transform your intention into reality and experience the *real* magic of life!

Step 3: Create the Portal of The LifeLine Technique Flow Chart is the doorway to the world of your reactive subconscious mind. Creating the portal is the last of the three *conscious*-mind components of the Flow Chart, and the number 3 of the 1-2-3 PLAN. It's important that every portal be specific to the Symptom-Stress → Intention that you've set (Step 2). To reinforce that concept, I use the mnemonic *P.U.M.P.,* which stands for Portal Used Matches the Possibilities (or perceived Problems). Most portals are based upon issues involving family, work, health, finances, and current events. These all mirror the patterns that exist within the subconscious mind.

Two Primary Portals

Every session with The LifeLine Technique begins with one of two primary portals: the *Conscious Mind Portal* or *Conscious Body Portal:*

106

— Regardless of whether the symptom you're experiencing is stress; addiction; limiting beliefs; phobias; self-sabotage; or any aspect of obsessive-compulsive thoughts, feelings, and behaviors, the **Conscious Mind Portal** will help manifest your intention. As you learned in *Step 2: Symptom-Stress → Intention,* the clarity of your intention is important.

Open your journal and review the intention you set. The Present-Past-Future Declarative Statement Portal uses that intention to acknowledge all aspects of your experience—where you are now (present), where you've been (past), and where you want to be (future). Creating harmony between the conscious and subconscious minds based on this portal will help you recognize your limitless potential.

— The **Conscious Body Portal,** on the other hand, is used for any discomfort or pain in your body, ranging from subtle to extreme. This portal reveals the subconscious, emotion-based patterns of reaction associated with these physical symptoms, as well as the root cause of why you've been unable to heal if the symptom is chronic. Keep in mind that the site or manifestation of the pain is *never* its actual source.

 **CREATE THE PORTAL**

Step 3: Create the Portal

The portal is the gateway or doorway to the subconscious mind. Look at Step 2 of your journal. The feeling from the intention you created—for example, "confident"—based upon imagining yourself living in the land of "I am filled with joy and laughter" is the positive intention that will be used to create the Conscious Mind Present-Past-Future Declarative Statements Portal. If your body is also speaking to you with a physical symptom, you'll be able to create a Conscious Body Portal as well. Depending upon the nature of the symptom or stress, you'll use the Conscious Mind Portal as your entry point and possibly the Conscious Body Portal.

Conscious Mind Present-Past-Future Declarative Statements Portal

MRT indicator muscle.   MRT "gives way."   ILS.

1. Based on the *feeling* from the intention from Step 2, recite the **Present-Time** aspect of the Present-Past-Future Declarative Statement: "I'm now *choosing* to feel _____."

(In the example, the intention was "I am filled with joy and laughter." The *feeling* was "confident." Use the *feeling* word in the above statement.)

2. After making this statement, use the bent-arm muscle-reflex test (MRT), saying aloud, "Hold strong." Check the MRT indicator muscle. If it "gives way," harmonize with the Infinite Love & Gratitude Sequence (ILS). Recheck the MRT indicator muscle and it should instantly "lock out." If it doesn't, harmonize with the ILS until it does.

3. Repeat the same Present-Time Declarative Statement: "I'm now choosing to feel _____ [e.g., confident]." Say aloud, "Hold strong." If the MRT indicator muscle "gives way" again, harmonize with the ILS. Continue repeating this statement and harmonizing with the ILS until the MRT indicator muscle "locks out" after saying the Present-Time Declarative Statement.

4. Now recite the **Past-Time** aspect of the Present-Past-Future Declarative Statement: "I'm okay that there is a part of me that has not been choosing to feel _____ [e.g., confident]." Say aloud, "Hold strong." Check the MRT indicator muscle. If it "gives way," harmonize with the ILS. Recheck the MRT indicator muscle and it should instantly "lock out." If it doesn't, harmonize with the ILS until it does.

5. Repeat the same Past-Time Declarative Statement: "I'm okay that there is a part of me that has not been choosing to feel _____ [e.g., confident]." Say aloud, "Hold strong." If the MRT indicator muscle "gives way" again, harmonize with the ILS. Continue repeating this statement and harmonizing with the ILS until the MRT indicator muscle "locks out" after saying the Past-Time Declarative Statement.

6. Now recite the **Future-Time** aspect of the Present-Past-Future Declarative Statement: "I am feeling _____ [e.g., confident]." Say aloud, "Hold strong." Check the MRT indicator muscle. If it "gives way," harmonize with the ILS. Recheck the MRT indicator muscle and it should instantly "lock out." If it doesn't, harmonize with the ILS until it does.

7. Repeat the Future-Time Declarative Statement "I am feeling _____ [e.g., confident]." Say aloud, "Hold strong." If the MRT indicator muscle gives way again, harmonize with the ILS. Recheck the MRT indicator muscle and it should instantly "lock out." If it doesn't, continue repeating this statement and harmonizing with

the ILS until the MRT indicator muscle "locks out" after saying this Future-Time Declarative Statement.

8. You can enhance this aspect of the portal by reciting the Future-Time Declarative Statement as "I am _____ [*feeling*—e.g., confident] because I am _____ [*intention*—e.g., filled with joy and laughter]." Check the MRT indicator muscle. If it "gives way," harmonize with the ILS. Recheck the MRT indicator muscle and it should instantly "lock out." If it doesn't, harmonize with the ILS until it does.

9. Repeat your intention with the Future-Time Declarative Statement by saying, "I am _____ [e.g., confident] because I am _____ [e.g., filled with joy and laughter]." If the MRT indicator muscle gives way again, harmonize with the ILS. Recheck the MRT indicator muscle and it should instantly "lock out." If it doesn't, continue repeating the Future-Time Declarative Statement and harmonizing with the ILS until the MRT indicator muscle "locks out" after stating your intention.

10. If your body is speaking to you with physical symptoms, follow the Conscious Body Portal instructions.

Next are the steps for opening a Conscious Body Portal.

Conscious Body Portal

Use your journal to help guide you with creating a Conscious Body Portal. Where is your body speaking to you with discomfort or pain? Allow yourself to tune in to your physical self as you open the Conscious Body Portal.

Now follow these instructions to create the Conscious Body Portal:

1. Touch the area of the physical symptom while using your other hand to perform the muscle-reflex test (MRT). If you're not able to reach the area of pain on your body, you can envision it while using the bent-arm MRT indicator muscle to activate it.

2. Say aloud, "Hold strong." If the MRT indicator muscle "gives way," harmonize with the ILS.

3. Recheck the MRT indicator muscle and it should immediately "lock out." If it doesn't, harmonize with the ILS until it does.

Walking and Breathing.

4. Challenge the painful area by walking in place and consciously breathing for 10 to 15 seconds.

5. Recheck the MRT indicator muscle, or reconnect to the painful area by consciously tuning in to it. Say aloud, "Hold strong." If the MRT indicator muscle "gives way," harmonize with the ILS. Recheck the MRT indicator muscle and it should immediately "lock out." If it doesn't, harmonize with the ILS again until it does.

6. Repeat the challenge of the portal by walking and breathing. Check the painful area again. Continue this process until the MRT indicator muscle "locks out" after walking and breathing.

Congratulations! You finished the 1-2-3 PLAN and have activated your subconscious mind's attractor field for manifesting your intention.

Now, pay attention to how it feels to be present in the moment. After performing the 1-2-3 PLAN, many people describe feeling lighter or more connected to the earth or Source. Whatever it is that you're feeling is okay. Your transformational journey has been activated and set into motion. The 1-2-3 PLAN's purpose is to guide the subconscious mind to take on the form and function of your intention. As a result, your body and the relationships in your life will begin to mirror your intention. Your nature is the intention that you've set; and as a result of performing the 1-2-3 PLAN, you won't be able to keep yourself from thinking, feeling, and acting from this mind-set. Run the 1-2-3 PLAN daily for 18 days and chronic challenges will dissolve before your very eyes!

Fear of Heights Is Now a "Love of Flying"

Gail Keeler is a Certified LifeLine Practitioner who lives near Boulder, Colorado. As she explains in her story (which she has given me permission to share with you), in order to achieve her dreams, she had to overcome a big fear:

> Throughout my life, I recall my mother saying, "No, I can't. . . . I'm afraid of heights." After learning The LifeLine Technique, I realized that I had subconsciously inherited my mother's fear. When I was 18, my mother and I flew from New York to Kent State University in Ohio. We were both terrified during the flight, although we did our best to comfort each other.
>
> Every time I flew after that, I visibly trembled whenever the plane took off from the airport. When there was turbulence,

I experienced sheer terror. I recall one time chatting with a gentleman seated next to me, hoping to distract myself from the massive, nonstop turbulence battering the plane. Suddenly, the plane dipped sharply. I screamed at the top of my lungs! On another turbulent flight I cried and recited the Lord's Prayer aloud nonstop. I was sure I was going to have a heart attack before the plane landed.

Despite the terror, I had to fly quite a bit for business. Then I decided to learn The LifeLine Technique, which meant I had to fly from my home in Colorado to Chicago. I said affirmations for days before flying—talking to myself and visualizing a safe, calm flight. But my body still felt like a car wreck on the inside. Then I went to my first LifeLine Technique training and experienced the most amazing healing and awakening work! I decided to run a LifeLine session on myself about flying. My intention was, and still is, "Every time I fly, I experience calm, peace, and joy in body, mind, and spirit." My flight home was amazing, calm, and peaceful, even though there was turbulence!

I conducted two more sessions with The LifeLine Technique, using my intention of being calm, peaceful, and joyful in body, mind, and spirit as part of the Conscious Mind Portal. The subconscious emotions that were released and harmonized during the session included anger, fear, resisting change, and inability to adapt.

Since those sessions, I haven't experienced any fear, nervousness, or anxiety when I fly. As a matter of fact, I now enjoy it![1]

The New Gateway for Healing

The gateway for healing with The LifeLine Technique is *Step 3: Create the Portal.* When you shift your focus from getting rid of symptoms or stressful experiences and recognize that they *exist solely as the vehicle to awaken you* to your limitless potential and power, you create inner peace. Once you remove the barriers to your perception of love's healing presence in your life, wrote

Gerald Jampolsky, M.D., in his book *Teach Only Love,* you're able to heal yourself on every level and in every way.[2]

The next chapters will discuss Steps 4 to 16. I'll explain the philosophy and science of the steps as we continue your mind's journey to inner peace. The exact explanation of how to run these steps is too detailed for the purpose of this book. Regardless, by following the 1-2-3 PLAN, you're activating a part of yourself that holds the power to heal, regenerate, and be whole.

⊕⊕⊕ ⊕⊕⊕

CHAPTER 16

Step 4: Time
to Create Balance

*"There are as many nights as days, and the one is just as
long as the other in the year's course. Even a happy life cannot
be without a measure of darkness, and the word 'happy'
would lose its meaning if it were not balanced by sadness."*

— Carl Jung

Before the era of digital recording, everything was on tape. Do you remember the 1970s television commercial with the late jazz diva Ella Fitzgerald in which a recording of her singing shattered a glass? At the end of the commercial, the announcer asked, "Is it live, or is it Memorex?"[1]

Whenever I think about that famous tagline, it reminds me of the subconscious mind. Because the subconscious is unable to distinguish between memory, imagination, or reality (the present moment),[2] whenever your body is expressing a symptom, it's a sign that an unprocessed subconscious memory has been activated. Consequently, your behavior, the physiology of your body, or your emotional response arises as if you're experiencing that subconscious memory for the very first time . . . again and again. Your responses replay every time you have similar emotional experiences that trigger the unprocessed subconscious memory. Over time, you become caught in a loop of physical symptoms and overwhelming stress; you're bewildered as to why your body and life are speaking to you in this way.

The truth is that every symptom and stressor is actually a subconscious Memorex recording. The activation of this recording has a direct impact on both your biology and your behavior. Your body becomes limited in its ability to consciously respond from the secure place of self-love and inner peace. As the tape continues to replay, it's impossible for your body to innately heal and regenerate as it is designed.

In *Hands of Light,* scientist and author Barbara Brennan says that imbalance is the result of forgetting who you are, which leads to not only an unhealthy lifestyle, but eventually to illness. Illness can thus be understood, she says, *as a lesson you have given yourself* to help you remember who you are.[3] Ultimately, if you remember who you are in each and every moment, every thought will be peaceful, every feeling passionate, and every action motivated by love.

Step 4: The Triad of Health

Step 4: The Triad of Health of The LifeLine Technique Flow Chart represents a subconscious reaction of imbalance manifesting as symptoms in your physical body, as well as stress in every relationship in your life . . . especially the one with the beautiful person you see each time you look in the mirror! The Triad actually refers to aspects of the *energetic* body—emotional, biochemical, structural, and spiritual (electromagnetic-field) reactions. It's triggered when an experience enters a subconscious state of resistance because you don't have the *conscious* tools, strategies, or support to deal with it in the moment.

EMOTIONAL ⟋△⟍ BIOCHEMICAL
SPIRITUAL
STRUCTURAL

In *Step 4: The Triad of Health,* you're seeking to determine *where* the subconscious reaction-based pattern of imbalance is located. Healing and thriving is a natural by-product of balance. Infinite Love & Gratitude is used to reconnect to your power and thus create harmony between your mind, body, and spirit. Once balance is restored, the body's natural ability to heal itself is unleashed.[4] Masaru Emoto notes in his book *The Miracle of Water:* "Only when love and gratitude are combined and balanced will they create a beautiful life for us, just as the combination moves the earth and the universe."[5]

In the next chapter, I'll provide an overview of *Step 5: The Power Center.* It's time to awaken to your power to live an intentional life!

⊕⊕⊕ ⊕⊕⊕

CHAPTER 17

Step 5: Awakening to Your Power

"For a shift in consciousness to be truly relevant,
it needs to be more than just intellectual or perceptual.
Each of us needs to take it into our hearts and our everyday lives.
We need to <u>feel</u> and <u>act</u> as though nature is conscious and sacred,
as though all human beings are part of one, interdependent whole."

— Edmund J. Bourne, Ph.D.

If you're searching for a book on how to change your attitude or mind so you can change your life, you have more than 40,000 titles to choose from on **Amazon.com**. Imagine—40,000 books! If the key to overcoming health challenges, bridging communication disputes, healing marital discord, or developing a positive attitude were as simple as studying a text or as easy as "making a different choice," would all those books need to exist?

It's a challenging, often painful time when searching for *the* way to change—looking for the *right* formula, the *right* book, the *right* teacher. The truth is that the "right" answer for each of us only exists *within*. What we need is the *right method* for bringing out the answers.

Making conscious, positive choices is very important, but that's only a small fraction of the equation. Self-discipline is one of the greatest catalysts for change. But symptoms and stressful responses to life represent repeated reminders of those parts of you that are out of reach of your conscious power of choice in the moment.

To create lasting change, you have to probe beneath the surface—get to the root causes of fear, stress, chronic pain, disillusionment, or any other negatively perceived aspect of life. Sustainable change can be likened to the difference between reading about driving a car and actually getting behind the wheel. Experience is the greatest teacher.

Moving in a New Direction

Hayley is a Certified LifeLine Practitioner who uses her background as an energy healer, dancer, and movement specialist to help clients release physical and emotional challenges that result in symptoms limiting their ability to move and experience serenity in their day-to-day lives. Hayley and her client Edward gave me permission to share this story:

> **Edward:** The Lifeline Technique has helped me far beyond anything that I thought was ever possible. I've had difficulty moving my right side and walking due to congenital cerebral palsy. There's always been an extreme difference between my right and left legs in terms of sensation and control, and there's diminished feeling in my right calf muscle and foot. I was most aware of the problem when I stretched at night or in the morning. As soon as energy passed through the right leg during the stretch, I developed muscle cramps. When I walked, the gait was also uneven.[1]
>
> **Hayley:** Using The LifeLine Technique Flow Chart, we discovered that the emotion channel of the Earth element wasn't flowing, which represented subconscious feelings of not being

supported, grounded, or nurtured. The spleen/pancreas meridian wasn't creating energy for the lung meridian. The cartilage in all regions of his body's structure was expressing the emotions of unworthiness and being oversympathetic. The subconscious emotions were being held in every area of his body, resulting in degeneration and a spirit holding pattern representing a moment of trauma in which there was a disconnection between Edward's body and mind.

After discovering the location of the assemblage point and bridging the gap between Edward's conscious and subconscious minds, the session with The LifeLine Technique ended with checking the Five Basics for Optimal Health. Edward needed to drink water more frequently, and he needed to own his power. I encouraged him to connect to his breath twice a day and give himself Infinite Love & Gratitude.[2]

Edward: What a difference the sessions have made! I immediately felt a difference in the way that I walked after each session. Today, I no longer feel any impairment in the way I move—the gait has vastly improved. For the first time in my life, both legs feel the same. The day after the third session, I felt excited and joyful! I never thought it was possible that I could have more movement in my right side! I believe the process of The LifeLine Technique opened my psyche—it released the blockage that I've been carrying around since birth. I feel freer in my body and more peaceful in my mind. I highly recommend The LifeLine Technique without reservation.

Awakening Your Heart

The process of change requires that you awaken and reconnect to your own thoughts, heart, and ability to choose the way that feels right—the subconscious powers of the mind. Addressing just the conscious aspects of these three primary ingredients will usually yield limited and oftentimes superficial change, leading you back to repeating those painful, scary, and stressful experiences again and again. ("Is it live, or is it Memorex?")

121

Awakening to your power is akin to a snake shedding a layer of skin or a caterpillar transforming into a butterfly . . . it's remarkable. This awakening isn't something that can be readily explained, written about, or even learned from watching a DVD; *it's an experience that's felt in the heart.* When you awaken to your power, every cell of your body experiences the pulse of that heart change; every cell vibrates with authentic soul power.

True power emerges when you stay present in a moment of pain, fear, or stress—no matter what the circumstances—and realize that love is the only choice. Beyond the complexities of the mind resides the simplicity of the heart . . . which only knows love. Dare to let go of who you think you are!

Step 5: The Power Center

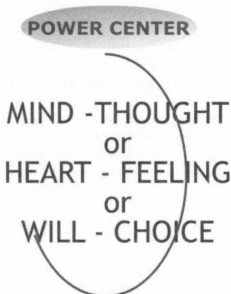

POWER CENTER

MIND - THOUGHT
or
HEART - FEELING
or
WILL - CHOICE

As noted earlier, once you've completed the 1-2-3 PLAN of The LifeLine Technique Flow Chart, the focus is the subconscious mind. While Step 4 represents a subconscious reaction of imbalance in your body or relationships in life (the Triad of Health), *Step 5:*

The Power Center represents an inability to maintain Present Time Consciousness (PTC) when facing a painful, scary, or challenging experience. This perception is expressed in the mind (thoughts), heart (feelings), or will (choice).

In Step 5, your goal is to determine what's *powering* the subconscious reaction of imbalance in your body or the relationships in your life (the Triad). The Power Center is an opportunity for you to recognize thoughts as a way to heal, feelings as a way to stay present in your body, and choices as a chance to love regardless of the circumstances. Once awakened to that power, your life becomes a passionate and mysterious adventure whose magic is discovered through embracing and accepting the journey rather than being identified or limited by any single moment.

When checking the Power Center, sometimes people become emotional without being conscious of why. For many of them, it's their first time being truly present, and connected with their power. The LifeLine Technique enables you to maintain an observer's view. From this vantage point, you can begin reframing the experience originally perceived by the conscious mind to be too painful, scary, or challenging to process into one that's not only positive, but also of meaning and value. How wonderful to recognize your authentic nature and power to live in the present moment! No matter how long the perceived negative pattern has existed, after completing *Step 5: The Power Center,* you're now ready to own your power!

The next chapter explores the meaning and lessons of challenging or negative experiences and why these lessons are so often hard to digest. *Step 6: The Spirit Protection Reflex (SPR)* of The LifeLine Technique Flow Chart brings into closer view the "gift" of the protective mechanism employed by the subconscious mind. Unwrapping it reveals your power for inner peace.

⊕⊕⊕ ⊕⊕⊕

CHAPTER 18

Step 6: The Gift in Strange Wrapping Paper

"It's kind of fun to do the impossible."
— Walt Disney

We never perceive the truth (the "here-and-now"); we only perceive what we believe. This paraphrase from the Torah, Judaism's founding legal and ethical religious text, expresses the transparency of declared truth—*we are all One; we are all pure love expressing ourselves the best way we consciously know how.* All roads lead to love.

Remember that the primary function of the subconscious mind is to maintain a sense of safety for the spirit when the conscious ability to choose love doesn't exist. I refer to this "safety" as the *Spirit Protection Reflex* or SPR. This reflex is an autonomic, automatic pattern of reaction that's activated by any one of the senses. The SPR occurs in a nanosecond and creates a gap of misperception between the conscious and subconscious minds.

The SPR represents another key difference between The LifeLine Technique and other systems of healing. What appears to be a negative experience of internalization, denial, disconnection, or loss is, in reality, what we refer to as the *Gift* . . . a moment of protection that graces you with the opportunity to learn, grow, and change in a way that you otherwise would have never known. It presents an opportunity for you to be honest with *yourself* and realize (with your *real eyes*) that there's a part of you that's been holding back from being your authentic self.

Spirit Protection Reflex/The Gift
Internalized, Denied, Disconnected, or Lost

Unwrapping the Gift

When the Spirit Protection Reflex's job is completed, symptoms and stress function as an alarm clock. Their intention is to get your attention and awaken you to your power. Like a candle illuminating a dark cave, the Gift of the SPR is that it is a signal to let you know you possess the ability to make a *conscious* choice to change your reality (the intention of Step 2) no matter what you or other people perceive that reality to be. Your spirit is now safe to authentically shine with loving thoughts, feelings, and actions.

In the book *Feelings Buried Alive Never Die . . .*, Karol Truman says that relishing an awakened state of consciousness is essential:

> Be enthused about becoming more aware of what you are feeling, of what you are thinking, of every word you speak, and of how you act or react in everything you do! Pay attention! Awareness causes results. When you become more aware of the challenges as they occur and see them for the opportunities they are, opportunities for growth—give thanks for what you are experiencing.[1]

Expressing gratitude is a major component of the healing process, especially as it relates to the Gift of the Spirit Protection Reflex (SPR). Gratitude allows you to recognize that you're not a victim of the symptom, experience, or stressor, but rather are being given an opportunity to start anew.

One of the people responsible for helping the allopathic medical community awaken to the importance of Love & Gratitude in the healing process is Bernie Siegel, M.D. In an essay on the value of gratitude, he wrote about the importance of physical and emotional pain for survival because they awaken us to care for our needs. He adds: "Being grateful for life, seeing it as an opportunity to give love, changes your life and allows you to live it as it is meant to be lived."[2]

Untying the Bow of the Gift

I completely understand the challenging nature of interpreting symptoms as a gift. It not only takes courage but great faith to view a diagnosis of cancer, heart disease, or any other degenerative process as something other than horrible. However, I'm offering you a way to listen and dialogue, revealing the *story of your soul.* With a humble heart, we each awaken to the meaning and value of our experiences.

I'd like to share with you Gloria's testimonial about her experience with The LifeLine Technique. Gloria and her husband, Bob, were among my first clients when I graduated from the National College of Chiropractic and worked in the office of Steve Ciolino, D.C., in Buffalo Grove, Illinois. They've both watched and been active participants in my evolutionary journey to help people transform their lives. Gloria explains:

> I think of myself as a vivacious, enthusiastic, energetic woman who enjoys a very healthy lifestyle. When people encounter me, no one can believe I am my "calendar age," which is 75 years young. They always assume I'm at least ten years younger. I am certain that my continual state of well-being can be attributed to Dr. Darren Weissman (whom I call Dr. W.) and The LifeLine

Technique, which Bob and I practice almost on a daily basis, as needed, for ourselves, family, and friends.

I haven't always been this healthy! In my 50s, I developed a multitude of allergies that included most trees, grasses, molds, wheat, corn, beef, pork, seafood, smoke, and cat dander. My joints swelled whenever I ingested nightshade vegetables (for example, potatoes), and I was also lactose intolerant. If Bob cut the grass and the windows were open, I could not breathe. I had to yell for him to assist me in closing up the house. We entered all restaurants tentatively, always armed with rescue inhalers in my purse, Bob's pocket, and the car. Several inhalers were also placed around the house.

I spent two hours with a nutritionist at a local hospital because I didn't know how to nourish my body without getting sick. At the end of the two-hour session, the nutritionist was as frustrated as I was. Her only guidance was to not eat "too many culprits at the same time."

In the spring of 1999, I was amazed to learn that Dr. W. could harmonize any allergy within 15 minutes without a shot or any invasive procedure. During that session, which was prior to Dr. W. awakening to The LifeLine Technique, he used kinesiology and some other modalities, such as Total Body Modification (TBM), to quickly isolate and harmonize the allergens. I returned home that evening to give my husband the news that I had homework—that night, I was to ingest every food that had been harmonized.

Bob had always enjoyed good health. He had never been to a chiropractor and was totally unfamiliar with kinesiology. Yet he was very interested in what had transpired and asked to be present at my next session.

After I did my homework, it would be a while before I needed another session. In the interim, Bob and I spent the best New Year's Eve of our lives—the new-millennium celebration—in a sometimes-smoky atmosphere. Although we carried inhalers in our coat and jacket pockets, they were never needed!

Over a period of time, I had several other health challenges— parasites and a lump in my breast. As Dr. W. expanded his breadth of knowledge, the sessions with him changed. I always felt much safer working with him than I did pursuing traditional Western medicine with the sometimes serious, organ-damaging side effects of pharmaceutical medication, or the risk of serious illness contracted during a hospital stay. I always experienced amazing results—for example, the suspicious-looking lump that was felt by my doctor and showed up on the first mammogram disappeared by the time I took the second!

Every time Dr. W. worked on me, I asked, "What are you doing?" Then I'd say aloud, "I want to know what you know." I think my constant prodding and questioning led to his decision to invite laypeople to the initial LifeLine Technique training in June of 2002.

I'll never forget the dark-field-microscope images shared by Dr. Tom Bayne during that first training. The microscope's image was projected on the screen, allowing all of the participants to observe the monumental visual changes in a drop of blood immediately following a session with The LifeLine Technique. Bob and I have attended many LifeLine Technique trainings since, always learning more as Dr. W. further developed the technique and shared his knowledge.

The most phenomenal experience I've had was in 2008. While on vacation, I experienced a bowel obstruction. I had it treated by an acupuncturist while in Florida. I promised to get a colonoscopy when I got home. Just before I was administered the anesthesia, the gastroenterologist asked about the symptoms. I explained how I had great difficulty emptying my lower bowel, despite the use of an entire container of suppositories in less than three months.

"That's not a GI problem," he replied. "You need to see a urogynecologist!" Nonetheless, the doctor continued the procedure. When I awakened, I still had the bowel obstruction, and even more questions.

My internist referred me to a urogynecologist. There was only one of these specialists in the entire county where I live, and his office was jam-packed with women when I arrived for my appointment. After a consultation and a very humiliating and invasive exam, I was told I had a rectocele, a weakening of the fibrous tissue in the rectum and vaginal areas. It's like a pocket in the vaginal wall, which caused the obstruction in the bowel. As I was to learn, this is a challenge for many postmenopausal women. Its cause is attributed to a weakening of the vaginal muscles due to a decrease in estrogen. But I knew, from my work with Dr. W., that there was an *emotional* reason why the muscles were weak in the first place.

The doctor recommended surgery, which would require several more painful and intrusive tests in preparation. In addition, I would not be able to do anything—no walking, no cooking, no activities outside my home—for 90 days after the surgery. As soon as I left the urogynecologist's office, I knew I needed to see Dr. W. ASAP!

When Bob and I arrived for our appointment with Dr. W., he asked one question: "Is there a tear in the vaginal wall?"

"No," I replied.

"Great," he said. "I vote for surgery!"

Bob and I were shocked into silence until he quickly added with a smile: "Let's do it right now! I've got a connection!"

It was one of the longest sessions with The LifeLine Technique that I had ever experienced. Like many of the previous sessions, the emotions were associated with my childhood. I was conceived during the Depression—the fourth child in my family. My mother was overwhelmed caring for her children under those stressful economic conditions, and she attempted to abort me. During the session with Dr. W., I was able to release the deep pain and resentment of the trauma I experienced during my childhood.

When the session was over, the results were phenomenal! The obstruction was gone, and I had normal bowel function. I felt so good that I forgot I had actually had surgery— "psychic surgery"—and I picked up a grocery bag that was too heavy. I had to return for another session a couple of days later, but I haven't had any problems since then!

Bob and I were able to enjoy a late-winter vacation that would not have been possible if I had proceeded to have conventional surgery. Today, my life is just as energetic and robust, filled with

Infinite Love & Gratitude for all of the gifts the universe has bestowed on me. Dr. Darren Weissman is right there at the top of the list![3]

Your Transformational Journey

Between the original moment the SPR was activated and the intention you set in Step 2 of The LifeLine Technique Flow Chart, you completed a transformational journey. The rite of passage of surrendering a part of you—while at the same time reclaiming another—is similar to the journey of a caterpillar becoming a butterfly. A part of you must be released in order for a new essence of your spirit to express itself fully. The SPR represents the gap of consciousness necessary for you to complete a transformational journey. Not until the caterpillar is in a state of utter darkness can the journey toward the light begin.

Harmonizing the Spirit Protection Reflex is akin to discovering the gift in your heart to live life with the consciousness of love. You could never imagine your truest nature while in a state of complete darkness, while at the same time the butterfly would never change the path it took to awakening to its destiny.

In the next chapter, you'll learn about *Step 7: The Five Elements,* which are synonymous with change. What's the change you're on the verge of making?

⊕⊕⊕ ⊕⊕⊕

CHAPTER 19

Step 7: Change . . .
a Natural Part of Life

"The human being is a microcosm of the universe, and so the description of the energy that activates the cosmos is the same description for the human being. We are Yin-Yang. We are Wood, Fire, Earth, Metal, and Water. Each of our organs is assigned to one of these elements . . . the pathways of energy within our bodies correspond to an element."

— Dianne M. Connelly, Ph.D.

Repeat after me: "I am now ready to change!"

You can do *anything* you set your mind to do! However, what does it really mean to "live your life in a state of 'be-ing'" or to "own your power"? Where does one begin the process of change, and how will you know you're actually in the process of "owning your power"?

I'd like to share the experience of Mary Beth Shannon, who was first introduced to The LifeLine Technique in 2007. She was one of the Certified LifeLine Practitioners who accompanied me to Australia in 2009. She shared the experience of her first LifeLine session in an e-mail:

My husband and I separated in March of 2007 after 26 years of marriage. We attended marriage-counseling sessions for six months, but we both arrived at the conclusion that we would divorce. Through a series of events—including the development of an intense rash all over my neck, throat, arms, and chest—my steps were divinely guided seven months later to the Hay House "I Can Do It!" conference in Tampa.

As soon as I entered the vendors' area at the conference, I first noticed your banner with the American Sign Language symbol "I love you" as part of the Infinite Love & Gratitude logo. I volunteer at the School for the Deaf and Blind, and when I saw your sign, I felt there was something at your booth that I needed to see. I talked to your wife, who told me all about The LifeLine Technique and suggested that I make an appointment.

Later that day, I had a session with a Certified LifeLine Practitioner named Steve Spencer. At the time, I couldn't even say "divorce"—I called it the *D* word—and thoughts of being alone were devastating. During the session with The LifeLine Technique, Steve instructed me to make the statement, "I'm okay getting a divorce." When I hesitated, he explained that in order to move forward in my life, I need to be okay with where I am now. He asked me to repeat the statement.

I nodded. It took a few moments and a few tissues to say the words, but I managed to get them out. When he muscle-tested me and my arm went weak, he said, "Infinite Love & Gratitude." Then he asked me to say aloud, "I'm okay being alone." That was really scary to say aloud, but I managed to say those words, too.

While I don't remember the details of the session, I do remember feeling calm and peaceful afterward. The next morning, 95 percent of the rash was gone!

I attended your talk that weekend; your message rang true to my soul, and I soaked up every word: "Being willing to change is the key to unlocking your limitless potential." At that moment, I knew I had to learn more about the power of Infinite Love & Gratitude. . . . I was ready, willing, and able to change![1]

The Metaphor for Change

Unlike Western medicine, traditional Chinese medicine views all aspects of the body as interconnected, and a change in one part impacts the harmony of the whole. The Five Elements in Chinese medicine mean *change*—these elements are the metaphorical representation of the change that occurs in your body and in all of the relationships of life. Understanding their meaning can help you appreciate the infinite universal power you possess to heal, regenerate, and be whole.

The Five Element Theory's history dates back to the 10th century B.C. It has been used to describe interactions and relationships in nature as a means to restore or maintain harmony. The art and science of feng shui harnesses the Five Elements to evaluate, restore, and maintain harmony in a home. Astrology calls upon this theory to observe the ebb and flow of one's life and therefore enable a person to predict or understand the nature of the experiences in it. My studies in the martial arts used different aspects of the Five Element Theory to recognize imbalance in an opponent and to enhance meditation and visualization practices. The LifeLine Technique uses the Five Element Theory to restore balance to the subtle emotional energy that feeds the body and optimizes the thriving nature of relationships.

Change is the one constant in life, even when you would choose something different. In her book *Life Changes,* Ambika Wauters explains why the lessons of change are invaluable to the healing journey:

> Change teaches us about the mystery of life and our part in its unfolding. As our potential is systematically transformed into a kinetic force that enhances our life force and takes us to higher ground, we become more of who we are.[2]

Nature is our mirror and, as I mentioned earlier, is a personification of Present Time Consciousness. It demonstrates the relationship between life and death, and the currents that travel between surviving and thriving, even when you're not conscious of it. If there were no changes, differences, or challenges, your potential for growth wouldn't exist or even be possible.

The Primary Elements of Nature

The Five Elements are *Fire, Earth, Metal, Water,* and *Wood,* which sequentially represent the primary elements of nature and the particular wisdom and power they metaphorically embody. They are synonymous with the same wisdom and power that you possess in your body and your life. Let's take a moment to explore the metaphorical expression of each of the Five Elements:

- The **Fire** element is activity, rising, life giving, and passion.

- The **Earth** element is mothering, nurturing, balance, groundedness, the Divine Feminine, and unconditional love.

- The **Metal** element is core stability, structural foundation, ability to bend without breaking, and discernment.

- The **Water** element is flow, movement, transformation, adaptation, and acceptance.

- The **Wood** element is growing, flourishing, rootedness, protection, flowing, and stillness.[3]

In Step 7 of The LifeLine Technique Flow Chart, the Five Elements provide you with the opportunity to connect to those parts of yourself that have been persistently resistant to change. When activated, the subconscious mind takes control. The Spirit Protection Reflex (SPR) will always override a conscious choice. The thought, feeling, or experience of an element represents the areas of your body and life where these subconscious patterns of resistance exist.

When conducting a session with The LifeLine Technique, observe the metaphors of the specific elements. They are the source of awakening consciousness. For example, if the element is Wood, there is subconscious *resistance* to growing, flourishing, or feeling rooted. Metaphors are commonly used to tell a story—they activate a part of the brain called the *corpus callosum.* The corpus callosum, explained in more detail in Step 14 of The LifeLine Technique Flow Chart, opens the bridge to the "conscious" aspect of the brain known as the *neocortex.* This enhances communication between the parts of the brain that are creative and logical. Creativity and logic are necessary to process and integrate information—enabling and enhancing memory, healing, and growth. Consciously connecting to the metaphor of the element enhances and expands your capacity to be the self-healing being of intelligence that you are.

Just as in life, the natural state of the elements is change. The movement associated with it exists in a both interdependent and complementary relationship. Because you're one with everything and everyone, your body and life are microcosms of those Five Element interrelations. For example, your relationships with other people can be passionate like the Fire element, nurturing like the Earth element, stable like the Metal element, flowing like the Water element, or rooted like the Wood element. Because of the duality—that is, positive and negative—of all things, your relationship with the elements also can be perceived as either the power of connection or of disconnection.

After harmonizing the Five Elements, you've unraveled another layer of the subconscious mystery that is the undercurrent of symptoms and stress inhibiting you from experiencing inner peace. In the next two chapters, which provide an overview of Steps 8 and 9, the significance of the power of the elements and change will become clear.

⊕⊕⊕ ⊕⊕⊕

CHAPTER 20

Step 8: Energy in Motion (E-motion) Stays in Motion

"Modern scientists puzzle why acupuncture points exist on the body surface. They were certainly not evolved for acupuncturists to insert needles! According to some modern workers the points, probably, form 'windows' on the body surface for exchange of cosmic energies, so that the body can remain in energy balance with the rest of the Universe . . ."

— Lord Pandit Professor Dr. Sir Anton Jayasuriya

Imagine you're on an airplane flying nonstop between New York and Los Angeles. Due to mechanical difficulty, your pilot announces that the plane will make an unplanned stop in Chicago. The emergency landing sets in motion a domino effect—some people will miss their connecting flights; others will be late to meetings; still others may miss a rendezvous with loved ones. Depending upon their individual perspectives, this will result in varying levels of stress for all passengers.

Like the emergency landing, when a subconscious emotional pattern of reaction is set in motion, the Gift of the Spirit Protection Reflex (SPR) occurs in the subconscious mind. There are multiple domino effects as a result—the most direct route of energy/

emotional flow from one acupuncture meridian to the next is interrupted.

Why is this significant? On a physiological level, the meridians carry energy, bringing vitality and balance to every single organ of the body.[1] When the energy flow is interrupted, this impedes the physical function of your body, or your ability to function optimally in your life. Suddenly, the domino effect spreads. Hopelessness, anxiety, slowing of the metabolism, depression, anger, high blood pressure, sadness, fear, autoimmune response, low self-esteem, blood-sugar imbalances, cravings for love and attention, inability to recognize cancer cells, vengeance, inflammation, vulnerability, feeling unsafe and defeated, or phobias are a few of the subtle ways that the lack of emotional flow through the meridians expresses itself.

When You're Ready to Heal

Certified LifeLine Practitioner Debra Hale is a massage therapist based in Arizona. She and one of her clients shared an experience that provided both of them with a profound lesson: when you're *ready* to heal, the symptom expresses itself. . . .

My client—I'll refer to her as Audrey—came to my office one afternoon for a healing massage. As I traced the meridians and massaged her legs, we discovered blockages affecting the fifth chakra, which is located at the throat. Using Infinite Love & Gratitude and The LifeLine Technique Flow Chart to create a balance in her energy centers, we discovered that something fearful and frightening had happened to her at the age of three. Audrey began to cry and felt as if she was in a very dark place. I told her I would go with her, and she would be safe. The crying stopped; she asked if it was important to remember what was so frightening. I told her no, her spirit knew, and explained that if it was necessary, she would remember. If not, it didn't matter.

Weeks later, Audrey and her family were planning a vacation to Hawaii. Her family decided to go scuba diving, but Audrey said she had always been claustrophobic and could not participate in that activity. As soon as she thought about being claustrophobic, the thought came: *You've healed from that.* Immediately, Audrey remembered the following experience, which she later shared with me:

> *I was watching my brother playing in a ditch when the ditch caved in on him and he was suffocating. My other brother told me to stop screaming and help dig or it would be my fault if our brother suffocated. I was only three years of age at the time.*

The LifeLine Technique awakened Audrey to the subconscious memory that manifested as the symptom of claustrophobia, which changed the quality of her life. The happy ending to this story: Audrey's brother was rescued from the ditch, *and* she was able to go scuba diving during her vacation. She told me she had a great time.

Audrey's experience reaffirmed to me as a practitioner the power of the subconscious mind to disconnect from an experience until we have acquired or developed the tools, strategies, and support for us to handle it.[2]

In Step 8, the symptoms "speak" as a lack of flow of energy or emotion through the organ-meridians.

The Body's Emotional Channels

In Chinese medicine, the life force that courses through the body's energy channels (acupuncture organ-meridians)—from the fingertips to the head, from the chest to the fingertips, from the feet to the chest, and from the head down to the toes—is referred to as *chi*. However, with The LifeLine Technique, we refer to those organ-meridians as *emotional channels;* and the life force flowing through those meridians as *emotion,* or *e-motion* (energy in motion). It's the energy that moves you.

In Audrey's experience, the primary emotion that was not flowing was fear, which resulted in the energy not flowing to the throat chakra (chakras are explained in more detail in *Step 12: Holding Pattern*), and her inability to fully experience her life (fear of scuba diving). Once those memories were harmonized with Infinite Love & Gratitude, even though she wasn't fully aware of their existence, she was free to make different choices.

Each of the Five Elements is associated with specific organ-meridians or emotional channels. There are 12 bilateral (meaning they flow on both sides of the body) emotional channels, whose flow is necessary for the healthy functioning of the corresponding organ. Let's examine these emotional channels and their connection to the specific elements:

- **Fire:** heart; small intestine; pericardium/sex organs; triple warmer, also known as the thyroid-adrenals

- **Earth:** spleen/pancreas; stomach

- **Metal:** lung; large intestine

- **Water:** kidney; bladder

- **Wood:** liver; gall bladder

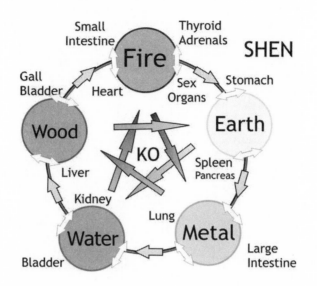

Feeling in the Moment

Do your best to develop a healthy and safe vehicle for expressing the emotions that you're feeling *in the moment.* As I'm sure you can attest, this is easier said than done. However, expressing emotion is essential, on par with breathing, drinking water, and sleeping. The more you're able to express yourself, the better you'll become at living true to yourself and treating yourself with love. The LifeLine Technique helps you discern and recognize those relationships, places, memories, or addictions that have become the catalysts for your awakening to your purpose and potential for inner peace.

In the next chapter, you'll learn about Step 9 of The LifeLine Technique Flow Chart—the cycle of the Five Elements—and why the cycle of emotion (e-motion) is important to the continuity of your life.

⊕⊕⊕ ⊕⊕⊕

CHAPTER 21

<u>Step 9</u>: Being Creative, in Control, and Whole

*"[The Five Element] cycles . . . are important because they identify
both change and regularity as constant features of life.
The passages of time, of journey, of growth, are changes laid
like melody over the rhythmic repeat of our natural cycles."*

— Gail Reichstein

Quantum physics reinforces what the ancient practitioners and barefoot doctors of Chinese medicine have always known—there's a singular web of infinite dimension that connects everything and everyone, everywhere, all of the time. Taking it one step further, I've discovered from my experiences with The LifeLine Technique that the fibers of this web are composed of emotion, the universal healing frequency of which is Infinite Love & Gratitude.

The flow of emotion—individually and collectively, from person to person, or from one nation to another—is analogous to how e-motion flows from one element to the other and from one acupuncture organ-meridian to the next. Like the rhythms of nature, our bodies and lives also follow that flow. This emotional connection, in Chinese medicine, is the cycle of the meridians—

known as *Shen, Ko,* and *Luo.* Noted author, acupuncturist, and teacher Dianne M. Connelly, Ph.D., says of the cycles:

> Constant interaction among the elements is what keeps us healthy, provided that each of the elements and functions within it are balanced. If one element is out of harmony, it is not long before the rest begin to feel the effects and go off balance."[1]

These cycles reflect the creative, controlling, and connecting energy and demonstrate the specific yet unique interaction, interrelatedness, and interdependence of the organ-meridians. When you examine the individual pathways of emotion, you appreciate the subtle but extraordinary power of change. Because e-motion is the energy that travels through the meridians, you see how all emotions are interdependent and interrelated in one way or another, a gentle reminder that they're necessary and are ultimately an expression of love.

There is a sense of mystery and metaphorical magic associated with the cycles—Shen, Ko, and Luo. With Step 9 of The LifeLine Technique Flow Chart, you're able to understand the way in which the cycle of the Five Elements correlates with what you're experiencing in both your body and life. Shen, Ko, and Luo are the mystery and metaphorical magic of creation, control, and connection.

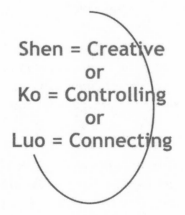

Shen = Creative
or
Ko = Controlling
or
Luo = Connecting

The Expression of Change

Shen is the creative.

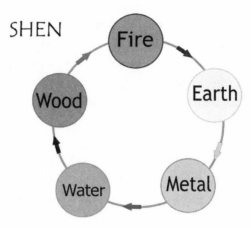

It reveals how the Five Elements express change. The element of Fire, for example, bears witness to the birth or creation of the universe, the big bang. From this moment of passion and inspiration, the element of Earth was born.

Deep within the core nature of Mother Earth, the simultaneous centripetal and centrifugal power of the Metal element was created—the same power that fueled the conception of the infinite universe. Metal represents the structural foundation of minerals that gives plants and animals alike the ability to stand erect and maintain their integrity, regardless of the pressure. Like a knife, the wisdom of Metal is one's ability to perceive from a place of core stability. Metal can bend without breaking; at the same time, when it's melted, it flows like molten lava. This is the birth of the element of Water.

Water's creation is flow, transformation, and acceptance. In the next instant, it moves on without attachment or looking back. Water holds no judgment. It's along this evolutionary journey that the seeds of infinite potential and physical life are activated, resulting in the birth of the Wood element.

From the depths of Earth, like an umbilical cord, the roots of the Wood element take form. The process of the journey to bridge heaven and Earth is born. Like the infinite universe itself, the seed grows in the only way it knows how—through darkness toward the light. At the moment when roots are healthy, strong, and stable, they break through the womb of Mother Earth. Rising like a rocket ship toward the sun, the Wood element, metaphorically represented by a tree, grows more powerful with every interaction. Seasons or storms stimulate the tree's enzymatic system, causing the roots to grow deeper, the bark to grow thicker, and the branches to reach higher.

When the Wood of the tree is rubbed vigorously together, a spark from the friction is formed and the element of Fire is born with a big bang. The infinite creative cycle of Shen is set into motion once again.

Let's take a deeper look at the Shen creative cycle with the following example.

In the Shen cycle, let's say that the Metal element is unable to create energy for the Water element. As you learned in Step 7 of The LifeLine Technique Flow Chart, the metaphor of Metal is core stability; and the metaphor of Water is going with the flow, change, or transformation.

When the Metal element is not *creating* e-motion for the Water element, you may feel unstable and unable to go with the flow. In other words, change makes you feel unstable.

Understanding the Power of Control

The *Ko* controlling cycle begins with the power of the Fire element controlling the Metal element, as in melting metal or forging a sword.

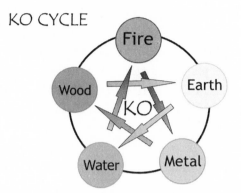

KO CYCLE

The power of the Metal element in Ko is control of the Wood element, as in the way an ax cuts down a tree.

The Wood element controls the Earth element, as in the seed of a tree developing and breaking through the surface of Mother Earth. The most complex wines come from grapevines that have had to work their way through the earth's soil to discover water on one end and sunlight on the other. It's a subtle yet powerful balance of control that guides and inspires—rather than breaking the will of—the element.

The Earth element controls the Water element by guiding or containing it with land. Without the banks of a river or a lake, Water's power and life have limited sustainability. Earth also controls Water by filtering out poisons and toxins.

The Water element controls the Fire element by extinguishing its flames. If there's not enough Water, Fire burns out of control. There's a healthy and necessary balance between each and every one of the elements.

The infinite Ko controlling cycle serves as a necessary check and balance for the Shen cycle. Each cycle is a new generation. The Shen represents the parents' creative connection to a child, while the Ko represents the grandparents' controlling connection to a child. For example, my late grandparents—Nana and Papa Kaplan, and Nonnie and Papa Ray Weissman—will always represent the sacred traditions of education and family that are the guiding principles of my life.

Like the Ko and Shen cycles, life's journey is guided and controlled through ancestral and generational relationships. Each time the elements traverse an entire cycle of the Shen or Ko process, a new and deeper view of oneself is revealed. Without the cycles of creation and control we'd stay the same, never evolving to understand the infinite possibilities available to each of us.

Reconnecting to Wholeness

The *Luo* connecting cycle represents the interdependence of the parts of an element within itself to experience wholeness.

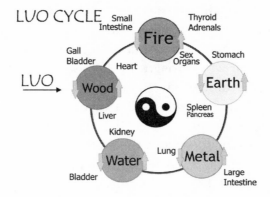

Like the Yin and Yang symbol, there's white on one side and black on the other. Within the white side there's a small dot of black, and within the black side there's a small dot of white. Each side has a primary purpose, anatomy, and function for the optimal flow of the whole.

The following is a list of primary Yin and Yang interrelationships. This is not a definitive list; however, it will give you an appreciation of how individual parts make up the whole.

Man and Woman   White and Black
Active and Passive   Up and Down

Solid and Hollow	In and Out
Fire and Water	Sympathetic and Parasympathetic
War and Peace	Love and Fear

All three of the cycles—Shen, Ko, and Luo—have their individual function and flow. The process, however, is simultaneous on both a micro- and macrocosmic level. Having an appreciation of the creative, controlling, and connecting cycles that exist within everything and everyone, all the time, is a huge step toward bridging the gap to create inner peace.

The seamless boundary of oneness appears most vivid in the shadows between light and dark. The simple truth is that every living and nonliving thing is composed of energy. Love and energy have one thing in common: they can't be created or destroyed . . . they just change form.

Seeing Beyond the Moment

The key to inner peace and the ripple it creates for the world is to go beyond the perception of what's right in front of you . . . to awaken to the mystery, magic, and miracles of creation, control, and connection.

In *Step 10: The Expression Channel,* you'll learn why the subconscious is expressing itself and what means it's using to share the message that you're ready to awaken to your spirit's highest vibration—inner peace.

⊕⊕⊕ ⊕⊕⊕

CHAPTER 22

Step 10: Expressing
Your Truth

"According to Indian spiritual traditions, disease is a vehicle whereby the truth of life and the truth of one's own self can be revealed."

— Barbara Brennan

Fear contracts and pushes away; it holds tight, and denies change or movement. Love, on the other hand, is expansive and all-embracing; it welcomes change as an expression of all life.[1] *Step 10: The Expression Channel* of The LifeLine Technique Flow Chart helps you appreciate how love is expressing itself the best way it knows how, and allows you to open your heart to embrace change.

The subconscious mind always overrides the conscious mind, and the Expression Channel operates as a primary spiritual feedback mechanism. It represents how your body or life is *literally* expressing subconscious emotions, either through behavior, physical symptoms, or the inability to fully communicate or release toxic levels of feelings. These expressions are also part and parcel of the belief system that grew out of these subconscious emotions, whose primary function is protection from anything painful, scary, or stressful. Under the cloak of these beliefs, pain and stress must be combatted, destroyed, dominated, ignored, or numbed; life must be lived defensively, cowering behind a wall of fear-based thoughts, feelings, and choices. This cloak inhibits you from perceiving the true nature and meaning of symptoms— a signal that it's time to dialogue, listen, appreciate, and change.

In many ways, the Expression Channel is the *source of the language of symptoms*. Like the diverse languages and dialects spoken around the world, subconscious patterns of emotion are expressed as myriad behaviors, physical imbalances, and unresolved feelings. These correspond to the Expression Channel area of The LifeLine Technique Flow Chart and appear in three forms: *emotional, structural,* and *biochemical.*

Think of yourself as a traveler in an unfamiliar land, seeking the services of an interpreter. Step 10 of The LifeLine Technique Flow Chart interprets *why* your body or life is expressing itself in the language of symptoms and explains *what* it's telling you. The answer to the "why" of the Expression Channel is: *for subconscious reasons.* The subconscious takes action as a means of protection. Consequently, it's important to acknowledge with gratitude this opportunity to know your truth.

At this point in the Flow Chart, I have my clients say, "Thank you! Thank you for protecting me; however, I'm now choosing to live my life intentionally, and this state of protection is no longer serving me for my highest good." The capacity to understand, forgive, accept, and have appreciation is directly connected to your ability to heal.[2]

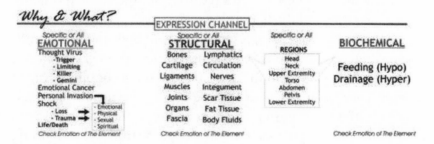

Understanding the Subconscious Protection

The components of the **Expression Channel** are:

- **Emotional Expression Channel:** Subconscious behavior

- **Structural Expression Channel:** Physical body expressing subconscious emotions

- **Biochemical Expression Channel:** Addiction to subconscious inability to feel, or let go of, feelings

The Emotional Expression Channel— the Subconscious Behavior Rules

Subconscious behavioral reactions are motivated by an innate survival instinct. These expressions of behavior are rigid, ritualistic, addictive, obsessive, and compulsive in nature. In the moment, they'll always override conscious choice. Consequently, subconscious cycles of behavior will continue to dominate your life until you become aware that the reaction represents a gap between the conscious and subconscious minds.

The different components of the Emotional Expression Channel are defined as follows:

— A **Thought Virus** is little different from a virus that wreaks havoc on your computer or that contributes to the breakdown of the physical body.[3] The primary distinction is that it's rooted in the subconscious mind. While the impact of Thought Viruses is outlined in detail in *The Power of Infinite Love & Gratitude,* for the purposes of understanding The LifeLine Technique Flow Chart, I'm providing an overview of *Trigger-, Limiting-, Killer-,* and *Gemini-*

Thought Viruses in this section.

Thought Virus behavior patterns are programs that infiltrate a person's mind as a means of subconscious protection. Just as a virus "impregnates" a cell and causes it to run the program of the virus, these incongruent, subconscious behavioral patterns replicate within the individual (host). Once the virus has taken root in your mind, because the mind is a microcosm of the macrocosm, it replicates internally and then impregnates new hosts externally in a "pandemic" way, infiltrating (sometimes quickly) the collective conscious mind. An example of that would be a crowd of people that suddenly becomes an unruly mob.

Rather than being "bad," however, Thought Viruses are Band-Aids protecting the conscious mind from what it's unable to perceive. They stay intact until you gain the ability to observe the experience through the eyes of love and compassion and have the tools to move through it with acceptance, forgiveness, and gratitude. Thought-viral symptoms hold a powerful potential for health and healing—once they're harmonized, the emotional immune system has been activated in a way that empowers behavior of your authentic self.

The following is an explanation of the four types of Thought Viruses:

1. **Trigger-Thought Viruses** are activated by any one of the senses.[4] Depending on which of the Five Elements is involved, when the virus is triggered, a particular subconscious behavior pattern is set in motion. For example, when you see the color blue, hear birds chirping, smell a flower, or taste something sweet, a sensory virus is activated. These simple, everyday experiences become an activating trigger of a subconscious behavioral reaction.

2. The **Limiting-Thought Virus**, when activated, sets in motion a subconscious behavioral reaction based on perceived limitations.[5] A common scenario for behavior impacted by a Limiting-Thought Virus includes thoughts, feelings, and actions

that express "I'm not good enough" or "If only I could be more." These patterns of rigid behavior pin you in a box; consequently, you settle into whatever is most comfortable and expedient in relationships, jobs, and health conditions, rather than going for a life driven by your dreams and passions.

3. When the **Gemini-Thought Virus**, what I refer to as the "clown face" virus, is activated, people look at you and see strength and courage; you radiate happiness. But on the inside, you're feeling timid, scared, and depressed.[6] The subconscious constantly shape-shifts as a means of survival when the conscious mind is unable to adjust.

The subconscious behavioral program of the Gemini-Thought Virus is an attractor field riddled with shame and guilt. When you're infected, you continually strive to be someone other than your authentic self. Your chameleonlike nature drives you to seek acceptance because you perceive the internal darkness of the Gemini-Thought Virus to be your truth.

4. The primary goal of the **Killer-Thought Virus**—a combination of mutated Trigger-, Limiting-, and Gemini-Thought Viruses—is to destroy the host. Once infected, you're triggered by everything.[7] You feel limited and helpless. When activated, the Killer-Thought Virus results in self-destructive behavior that includes thoughts, feelings, and actions driven by intense self-hatred. From the outside, it either looks like slow suicide or reckless abandonment. War is a widespread Killer-Thought Virus that has mutated out of control within the subconscious mind of all of humanity. In reality, Killer-Thought Virus patterns are similar to a "Mission Impossible" assignment that self-destructs once the agent has read or heard the instructions.

— **Emotional Cancer** is a mutated emotion that stems from the subconscious mind, rather than the physical body.[8] For example, anger becomes rage, anxiety becomes panic, or fear becomes terror.

Through the symptoms and behaviors that are manifesting as Emotional Cancer, the subconscious mind is signaling that you're now ready, willing, and able to be your authentic self.

Emotional Cancer doesn't mean that there's cancer of the physical body, just like the MRT indicator muscle that gives way with gall bladder or liver meridians doesn't mean that the person has gall bladder or liver disease. Emotional Cancer is an energetic version of the growing medical field of *psychoneuroimmunology*—the study of the interaction between psychological processes, the nervous system, and the immune system. It's a signal that it's time for a dialogue and a reconnection to Source. Emotional Cancer ultimately represents a subconscious reaction that influences one's behavior.

People frequently change who they are for the sake of others, at the expense of themselves. After a while, they've changed/mutated themselves so many times that they no longer recognize who they are. Even looking into their own eyes in the mirror becomes painful; they no longer recognize the person they're seeing. This is the core of spirituality: "Who am I?"

Whenever we change who we are for the sake of being accepted, we lose the infinite capacity and power to shine. The truth of who we all are is pure love. The increasing numbers of diagnoses of physical cancer is a direct link to how far away humanity has strayed from its connection to the spiritual truth of life itself.

— **Personal Invasion** shows up on The LifeLine Technique Flow Chart when a person doesn't feel emotionally, physically, sexually, or spiritually safe and is unable to express free will.[9] These boundaries are tied to individual values, beliefs, and perceptions; and are subconscious patterns of behaviors received from the environment. Patterns of behavior on a subconscious level that stem from Personal Invasion will have a direct impact on every relationship in your life. This can range from someone rummaging through papers on your desk at work to feeling emotionally, physically, or sexually bullied.

Because of the interconnection and interdependence of all subconscious minds, Personal Invasion is a collective experience. When one person is fighting, we're all at war . . . a war of the mind, heart, family, and world. We know from history that this isn't an effective means of reconciliation. Peace is achieved one person at a time—one person with an open heart, authentically expressing his or her power and knowing all is well.

— When an experience goes beyond your conscious ability to adapt, the subconscious mind is individually and collectively designed to protect itself by going into a state of **Shock**, which can occur as a state of loss or trauma and manifests on an emotional, physical, sexual, or spiritual level. It results in an inability to feel.[10] The loss or trauma is experienced energetically by the heart and eventually leads to a complete shutdown. Consequently, the heart system is unable to circulate lifeblood for healing and wholeness. Cardiologists are modern-day warriors for healing the battle scars of the heart.

Just like the iris around the pupil in the eye will constrict to protect the eye from receiving too much light, the heart has a protective barrier that restricts the flow of feelings to and through it. This mechanism of protection is associated with the subconscious behavioral pattern of shock. Heart attacks, congestive heart failure, and other heart diseases are among the most common causes of death in the world. However, long before the physical heart is damaged, the energy of the heart is blocked by shock.

— In an infinite universe, there's no such thing as death, only life in many different forms. Death appears when you observe the world through the lens of duality. The **Life/Death Mode** of subconscious behavior represents an *identity* that's ready to die. A part of you is prepared to let go with grace and ease, just like the leaves in autumn naturally fall from a tree after they express their full potential.[11] Now is the time for you to express the season of spring . . . to give birth to new buds and blossoms of hope, inspiration, and intention. The seasons of nature are naturally flowing through you in each and every moment. The LifeLine Technique gives you the opportunity to live fully and let go completely. Each moment is both a death and a birth, a ritualistic ceremony and a rite of passage—surrender to the beauty of each and every moment.

The Structural Expression Channel— Your Body Speaks Your Mind

The physical body is composed of individual cells working together for a common cause—the symphonic expression of oneness. Each of these cells is guided by e-motion flowing through the emotional channels (organ-meridians) of the Five Elements. As a result, there's an attractor field guiding the formation of physical expression based on how we emotionally flow through life, and how life emotionally flows through us.

The different components of the **Structural Expression Channel** are:

Bones	Cartilage
Ligaments	Muscles
Joints	Organs
Fascia	Lymphatics
Circulation	Nerves
Integument	Scar tissue
Fat tissue	Body fluids

When the Structural Expression Channel is activated, specific or all aspects of the physical body are expressing subconscious emotional patterns of reaction, such as muscle or joint soreness or slow circulation. It's easy to get caught up in the pain of the body . . . pain has a way of getting your attention. However, the Structural Expression Channel helps you recognize how the physical self is a vehicle for the *subconscious* expression of emotions that at one point you didn't have the ability to express. Rather than being victimized by the body, be aware that discomfort, numbness, fatigue, and pain are the first steps toward bridging the gap between the conscious and subconscious minds. Once they're bridged, healing and wholeness are the natural by-products.

In Eckhart Tolle's consciousness-raising book *A New Earth,* he refers to the *pain-body*—a subconscious conversation expressing itself through the physical body.[12] Tolle notes that this is the ego's way of expressing emotion in order to maintain a particular egoic identity; it uses the physical body as a means of subconsciously expressing emotions for that part of ourselves that at one point was unable to be in a state of power.[13]

The journey of your life takes on a whole new meaning and the road to inner peace is clear when you remember that all pain, fear, and stress are subconscious expressions of emotion based upon protection and learning.

The Biochemical Expression Channel— Understanding the Expression of Feelings

There's a particular subconscious emotional memory at the root of all addiction. It's an experience that either leaves you feeling empty or overwhelms you with pain and anguish. When triggered on a subconscious level, this rush of emotion results in a reflexive reaction of desire, longing, and desperation for a state of inner peace and wholeness. Addiction on a physical level represents a chemical dependence on a substance or an experience outside of oneself. It's this substance or experience that activates the production of an emotional state within the physical cells of the body all the way down to the genetic expression of who you are. It's easy to get caught in the mousetrap of addiction, blaming the substance or the experience for the pain, fear, and stress. However, the addictive substance or experience is merely an activating pattern, stemming from a part of you that at one point didn't have the ability—like you do now—to own your power.

On the subject of emotional addiction, Joe Dispenza, D.C., wrote in his book *Evolve Your Brain:*

> We have all experienced emotional addiction at some point in our life. Among its symptoms are lethargy, a lack of ability to focus, a tremendous desire to maintain routine in our daily life, the inability to complete cycles of action, a lack of new experiences and emotional responses, and the persistent feeling that one day is the same as the next and the next.[14]

The truth of addiction is that you long to shine at your highest vibration and be your best self, but a part of you is afraid. This is the part of you that—due to limiting beliefs—desires and longs for a way to internalize, deny, and disconnect from feelings as a means to survive. The pain you experience in your body is no different from the pain you experience in your heart. Life is a journey of addiction to food, e-mail, cigarettes, alcohol, street drugs, prescription medications, clothes, politics, chocolate, religion, media, coffee, attention, cars, bingeing, purging, war, shoes, clutter, purses, approval, jewelry, self-help, pain, shopping, doctors, celebrity gossip, power, and on and on. These addictions are all meaningful and hold value, depending upon one's perspective.

Addiction ultimately represents a gap of consciousness. The subconscious and conscious minds are being tethered between two separate times and places from one single moment. Unless that gap of consciousness is bridged, the Biochemical Expression Channel will find another route to express itself. That's why addiction is so pervasive on both an individual and collective level. Street or prescription drugs will transform into sex addiction. The addiction to greed and oil will transform into further oppression of human rights. Harmonizing the individual and collective perceived emotional patterns of emptiness or overwhelm with Infinite Love & Gratitude is the way you'll begin to transcend addiction and transform it into the light of free will and divine willpower.

The Biochemical Expression Channel opens the door to emotional freedom on your journey to inner peace. It will lead you along the subconscious path to living in Present Time Consciousness (PTC) and leading an intentional life. It represents the subconscious conversation stemming from the perceived need to monitor or suppress an authentic expression of feelings.

There are two components of the Biochemical Expression Channel:

1. **Feeding** (deficiency of emotion): If the Biochemical Expression Channel needs to be fed, the heart is closed and emotions must be *felt.*

2. **Drainage** (excess of emotion): If the Biochemical Expression Channel needs to be drained, the heart is wide-open, causing an excess of emotion that must be *released.*[15]

Self-Treatment Relieves Creative Blocks

Before becoming a Certified LifeLine Practitioner in July of 2009, Kathleen was experiencing symptoms of creative block. She sent me an e-mail to share her experience:

> I was creating a Web page, struggling to find the right words and create the best possible layout. Finally, at 11 P.M., believing I wouldn't be able to get it to work out the way I wanted, I gave up and decided to go to bed. As my head hit the pillow, I said to myself: "You will never get it right; why even bother!"
>
> Immediately, a sharp pain shot through a toe on my left foot. I attempted to find a comfortable position, but no luck. I used a progressive relaxation technique that normally helped me drop into dreamland. But *Toe still hurts!* flashed through my brain like a neon sign. I decided I needed to get out of bed and conduct a session with The LifeLine Technique.

My initial intention was simple: I wanted to make my toe feel good again so that I could sleep. Then as I thought about it, I added that I wanted to also release the despair I was feeling before it formed a new creative block.

Using an advanced LifeLine Technique portal known as the Core Limiting Belief, I discovered that the energy wasn't flowing through the second chakra. It was no surprise to me that this chakra represents creativity, among other things. I smiled as I put on the corresponding orange chakra glasses [the meaning of these is explained in Chapter 24]. I checked to see which of the Five Elements needed support. The indicator muscle gave way on Wood—which has to do with feeling rooted and protected. The emotion was "overwhelmed." When I checked for an original occurrence, it was age 42.

I immediately reconnected to the experience—at age 42, I was working at a software start-up company in a one-person marketing department. No matter what I did, I couldn't please my boss. As I harmonized those feelings of being overwhelmed with Infinite Love & Gratitude, the pain in my toe began to melt away. I completed the session using The LifeLine Technique Flow Chart. Not surprisingly, when it got to the Expression Channel, which explains what way the body is expressing the subconscious emotion, "structural" and "bones" in the lower extremities came up. By the time I finished the session, the pain had greatly diminished.

As I was folding up my LifeLine Technique Flow Chart, I glanced at the back cover where the gall bladder meridian is illustrated. I noticed that the meridian ended in the toe that was speaking with sharp pain and that the time it is most active, which is known as its *circadian rhythm,* is 11 P.M. to 1 A.M. I know I shouldn't have been surprised, but I was! As simple as this session was, it was great confirmation that The LifeLine Technique works the way it does for *definitive* reasons. Not only is my toe back to normal, but my creativity is flowing better than ever![16]

Step 11: Check Emotions is the crux of The LifeLine Technique. In the next chapter, you'll learn how to discover the emotion(s) that triggered the subconscious mind to react with the Gift of the Spirit Protection Reflex (SPR). With the discovery of the emotion(s) being kept under wraps, the story of the symptom takes on a new dimension of clarity, and with it, a deeper understanding of what it means to live in peace.

⊕⊕⊕ ⊕⊕⊕

CHAPTER 23

Step 11: Emotions, the Energy That Moves You

"The main thing is to feel emotion, to love, to hope, to quiver to live."
— attributed to Robert Henri

E-motion is the subtle driver of life and propels every aspect of who you are. Your thoughts, feelings, and actions are fueled by, and are the ultimate representation of, the energy that moves you. Most people are so immersed in subconscious emotion—like a fish in water—that the vast majority of the time they're unaware that it is propelling them through all of their experiences. In his book *The Divine Matrix*, Gregg Braden writes that we're all a part of one big web:

> There is a field of energy that connects all of creation. . . . This field plays the role of a container, a bridge, and a mirror for the beliefs within us. The field is nonlocal and holographic . . . each piece mirrors the whole. . . . We communicate with the field through the language of emotion.[1]

We know from the laws of physics that energy in motion (e-motion) stays in motion unless met by another force. When emotion is authentically expressed, the spirit of pure love is free to soar. What gets in the way of emotion flowing freely? On a conscious level, it's judgment. We assign the labels of "good," "bad," "wrong," and "right" to every experience, when the truth is that *all emotions are good*. This is a *spiritual* perspective based on the concept of duality, or as described by Buddhists, "the oneness of good and evil." Think of Yin and Yang, light and dark, or up and down—neither is solely good or solely bad. It all depends upon your perspective in the moment.

The LifeLine Technique is the quantum-healing technology that helps bridge the gap between what you may perceive as a negative emotional experience and a positive emotional intention for transforming your life. The by-products of bridging this emotional gap are healing, thriving, and an awakened passion for living. You have the potential to shift away from a primary belief that says "Life is happening to me" to an awakened *knowing* that you are the "co-creator" of your life.

The Gift of an Injury

David and I have been best friends since we were 13. We met at an overnight camp and have remained close ever since. We were roommates in college and served as best man at each other's weddings. David's dogged persistence and self-confidence, irrespective of the obstacle, are among the things I greatly admire about him.

At least two or three times per week, we get together to play tennis, and David brings that dogged persistence to the court. During the more than 20 years we'd been playing tennis together, however, he'd never won an entire set. We actually began betting $5 each match, then making each game "double or nothing." The sum of money David owed me was greater than the U.S. national debt . . . trillions.

One day I hit a solid backhand return as David set up for his forehand. The next thing I knew, he had screamed and fallen to the court, writhing in pain while holding the back of his heel.

"Who threw a ball at my heel?" he yelled.

I knew exactly what was going on because the same thing had happened to me eight years before while playing tennis: David had ruptured his Achilles tendon. He was unable to put any pressure on his right leg, so he leaned on me as I guided him to the bench at the side of the court. I began to conduct a quick session with The LifeLine Technique, starting with the Conscious Body Portal. I made it quick because I was running late to see clients. I happened to have a far-infrared magnetic wrap and several magnets in my gym bag, which I loaned him. I knew they would support the healing process.

After the first session, David was able to drive home. Later he met me at my office for one more. I'm not sure where the session actually took him—I was in the zone—but in Chinese medicine, the Achilles tendon is associated with the Water element. I recall that David, who manages a large team for an international conglomerate, was experiencing some stress at work. When we finished the session, he was able to put more pressure on his foot.

The next day I called to check on David. He told me he was feeling better and was able to get around more easily. He asked if it was okay for him to go on a business trip the following day. I encouraged him to listen to his body.

David called me from his business trip in South Carolina. "You'll never believe this," he said. "I can walk perfectly on both legs without pain!"

Two weeks later, David said he felt good enough to go back to playing tennis. He played his best match ever, and for the first time in 20 years, he beat me! The amazing part of this story isn't that David healed in two weeks from a ruptured Achilles tendon, even though this type of injury can take six to eight months to heal. Rather, as a result of the symptom (the injury), he was able to create an entire new neural network that enabled him to think, feel, and act with even more dexterity, balance, and confidence. The saying that the body "speaks" the mind holds true when the mind is bridged with Infinite Love & Gratitude—the person's body and life heal on all levels.

I was even more excited than David when he outplayed me. However, it didn't stop me from taking back the trophy the following week! David has won a handful of times since, and we continue to play for double or nothing on a regular basis.[2]

Processing: As Important as Eating

With *Step 11: Check Emotions* of The LifeLine Technique Flow Chart, the goal is to discover and harmonize the emotions at the root cause of the subconscious patterns of reaction. Processing them is as important as eating; and it's similar to the way you digest, metabolize, and assimilate food.

Step 11 transforms The LifeLine Technique Flow Chart into a laser, discovering and interpreting the emotions that are consuming you on a subconscious level . . . emotions that ordinarily you wouldn't be aware were present if it weren't for the varying levels of pain, fear, or stress in your life. This evolving level of consciousness helps you appreciate and recognize the power of the subconscious mind. Who could ever imagine that in the midst of uncomfortable, insecure, and stressed-out behavior or physical symptoms resides the lesson that you have limitless potential and infinite power? Symptoms are the catalyst for your evolutionary journey to awaken—the power to heal exists within each and every one.

Always Do Your Best to Choose Love

One of the challenges I've noticed since the world has awakened to the law of attraction is the judgments and guilt associated with challenging or stressful experiences. "I must have done something wrong to get cancer, go through a divorce, or have my child commit suicide . . ." (Press "record" in your subconscious mind—I'm making an enormous point right now.) Just because you didn't consciously choose a moment doesn't mean that you don't have to take responsibility for your life. Remember, it's not what happens to you, but rather how you *respond* to what happens.

Always do your best to choose love. Shawn Gallaway, whose song I mentioned in Part I, wrote "I Choose Love" in response to the events on September 11, 2001. In a moment of collective terror, panic, and rage, Shawn chose love. If you have Internet access readily available, please take a moment now to go to the Website **www.shawngallaway.com** and watch his "I Choose Love" video. There's a Chinese proverb that aptly describes his work: "A picture's meaning can express 10,000 words."

Let's proceed to the next chapter to learn how symptoms can sometimes be locked in a continuous loop of imbalance known as *Step 12: Holding Pattern.*

⊕⊕⊕ ⊕⊕⊕

CHAPTER 24

Step 12: The Key to Healing, Regeneration, and Wholeness

"Every experience that is drawn through any of the senses . . . has an effect on one's health."

— Sri Sathya Sai Baba

We often hold on to the residual emotions of an experience in the form of anger, fear, resentment, frustration, and anxiety. Those emotions continue to churn long after the experience has concluded. The actress Carrie Fisher once wrote: "Resentment is like drinking a poison and waiting for the other person to die." Holding on to emotion, not expressing what is in your heart, can cause a toxic or poisonous state for your mind, body, and spirit.

What's the root of the pattern of holding on—of being physically or mentally unable to let go? In The LifeLine Technique Flow Chart, this process is referred to as *Step 12: Holding Pattern.* Like a tornado emerging in the midst of a thunderstorm, it's a whirlwind of uncontrollable energy. It holds the potential for devastating destruction, and at the same time, for transformation and creation.

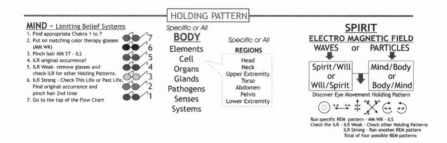

Peace for Veterans

On Infinite Love & Gratitude (IL&G) Day, June 18, 2009, the entire LifeLine family offered free sessions to U.S. military veterans throughout the nation. It is a tradition we intend to carry out every year. Sharon is a recently certified LifeLine practitioner based in North Carolina whose gentle compassion warmly engulfs everyone with whom she works. She sent me an e-mail to share her IL&G Day experience:

> One of the veterans with whom I worked was an Army medic. When I asked him what he would like to work on, he told me that he was experiencing depression, sadness, and frustration. On a scale of 0 to 10, 10 being excruciating, he ranked the feelings between 6 and 7.
>
> As the session with The LifeLine Technique proceeded, the veteran had numerous layers of the emotion "no right to exist" that we harmonized with Infinite Love & Gratitude. He never shared any details with me during the session; he kept everything very close to the vest. When we finished, I asked him to connect, and compare how he was feeling now with how he felt before the session. He was surprised to realize that those feelings of depression, sadness, and frustration were now 0. He even attempted to connect to the original feelings, but he couldn't.[1]

The Peace to Let Go

Step 12: Holding Pattern in The LifeLine Technique Flow Chart allows you to experience the peace of fully letting go of an experience—whether it's tied to a person, place, memory, or addiction. It's in this process that you're able, for the first time, to truly perceive the experience's infinite nature and the value of your having had it.

There are three aspects of the **Holding Pattern:**

1. **Mind Holding Pattern:** Limiting belief systems

2. **Body Holding Pattern:** Degeneration of the physical body

3. **Spirit Holding Pattern:** Trauma in the electromagnetic field

Each of these holding patterns, which will be detailed separately in this chapter, has a unique way of protecting the spirit while simultaneously providing major opportunities for learning and wholeness. Anytime a holding pattern is present in your subconscious mind, there's a complete misperception of yourself and the relationship you have with the environment. This lens of misperception affects your behavior, choice of words, and internal dialogue.

At the same time, because we're all holographic in nature and emotion is the bridge connecting everything and everyone, our cells mimic that same misperception. Hence, the body mirrors the subconscious misperception and operates from that same point of view. This creates stress both individually and collectively for the cells. The lens of misperception makes it difficult, if not next to impossible, for the body to adapt to any environment so that it can effectively and efficiently metabolize energy, detoxify itself, maintain immunity, sustain hormonal balance, and operate every other system.

Misperception of the Divine Feminine

One of the most obvious holding patterns impacting all of humankind is the misperception of Divine Feminine energy, which manifests in how we treat our planet, Mother Earth, as well as ourselves. The blame; shame; guilt; and denial of the wisdom, power, and beauty of women are a primary expression of those subconscious emotional patterns of reaction. While we all know that religious, political, economic, and social institutions have historically oppressed and suppressed the Divine Feminine, I believe the genesis of this oppression and suppression has been completely misunderstood.

For those of you who play the game of chess, you'll recognize that the queen is the most powerful piece. She is able to move across the chessboard more freely than any other. The king, on the other hand, is often believed to be the most powerful chess piece because once he is lost, the game is over. But the king is only able to move one space at a time, methodically hiding throughout the game in an attempt to survive.

There is a point in a chess match when sometimes it's necessary to *sacrifice the queen* as a means to win the game. This sacrificial act is at the heart of the drama of the chess game, and it mirrors what humankind is now facing—a mechanistic worldview, coupled with a reactive lifestyle, scurrying from moment to moment in an attempt to survive the onslaught of perceived attacks.

Many of us are like the chess piece known as the pawn: moving one moment at a time, easily sacrificed, and rarely recognized for our unique value and purpose. However, the pawns' arduous trek across the chessboard to reclaim the queen is a rite of passage and a tipping point where pain becomes power, fear dissolves into courage, and stress becomes the motivating factor to turn within and shine even brighter. The journey of the pawn in chess is similar to the one we must all undertake to reawaken to our power, versatility, and inner potential to thrive. The exchange of a pawn for a queen represents how one person can truly make a difference if that individual dares to dream.

The fate of Mother Earth and the peace of the entire planet now rest with those of us willing to do whatever it takes to "reclaim the queen." The first step is to shift our gaze away from those religious, political, economic, and social institutions in search of answers, and instead turn our sights within. We must embrace the holographic relationship we have with our queen, Mother Earth, and recognize that the effect of our ultimate disconnection from love—global warming—is also the ultimate disconnection we have within ourselves . . . from self-love.

Recognizing Our Need for Love, Nurturing, and Balance

Divine Feminine energy radiates outward from the heart; it is unconditional, compassionate, nurturing, helpful to others, and receptive—in other words, the principles that constitute the very definition of peace. The separation from the Divine Feminine is a crisis that we're all experiencing, but I'm seeing it especially with female clients.

With permission from my client, I would like to share with you one such experience. It also includes all 16 Steps of The LifeLine Technique Flow Chart so that you can get a better picture of what a session entails:

> Colleen is a highly successful professional who loves to sing and dance. At the same time, she wrestles with issues of self-worth. She wants to have a relationship, but is conflicted by her limited perceptions of her body. In many women, conflicts revolving around the struggle to understand and embrace both the power and sacred covenant of the Divine Feminine manifest as menstrual issues. The energy of the sex organs is passion, creative expression, and the internal process of giving birth to who we're meant to be. Colleen's body was "speaking" to her with the symptom of severe menstrual cramps.
>
> The LifeLine Technique session with Colleen began with making sure that her body, mind, and spirit connections were

upgraded and in harmony with the field of the earth and Source **(Step 1)**.

Familiar with the process, Colleen immediately told me that her intention **(Step 2)** was to make some changes in her life.

"Of course, I no longer want these physical symptoms," she said. "But I also want to make some deep shifts in my life, and I truly want to have a relationship."

It's important, when setting an intention **(Step 2)**, to be as specific as possible. As a LifeLine practitioner, I have a goal to help clients shape the intention *toward* love rather than merely getting *away* from fear.

"To get the most out of this session," I explained, "it's important that your intention focus on where you're going rather than where you no longer want to be. Imagine yourself waking up tomorrow feeling great about your life, about yourself; and basking in the 'deliciousness' of an authentic, reciprocal, committed, and intimate relationship. . . . How would you emotionally *feel* if that were to happen?"

Colleen's smile was infectious. It made me chuckle. "My heart would be beating with joy!" she exclaimed, momentarily dancing.

"Great! Then your intention is to have your heart beat with joy!" And I knew that the by-product of this intention would be that her body and life would no longer need to speak to her with the symptoms of menstrual pain and relationship stress.

I'm going to share with you some of the steps of The LifeLine Technique Flow Chart that will provide you with an interpretation (albeit a bit advanced) of The LifeLine Technique session I conducted with Colleen so that you can appreciate all aspects of the web of oneness and the subtle ways the subconscious mind uses to "speak with symptoms":

I used the Conscious Mind Portal Declarative Statements **(Step 3)** to begin the process of bridging the gap between Colleen's conscious and subconscious minds. There was an emotional and biochemical imbalance in the Triad of Health **(Step 4)**. Colleen disconnected from her power to feel and denied her ability to choose and take action **(Step 5** and **Step 6)**. The session took us to the Water element **(Step 7)** in a Ko cycle where the kidney **(Step 8)**, whose energy stores toxic loads of emotions, was unable to control the energy flow to the sex organs **(Step 9)**.

The Biochemical Expression Channel **(Step 10)** of drainage meant that she was unable to let go of the subconscious emotion of "helpless" (Emotion #18 in the Water element/**Step 11**) to a point where it had reached poisonous and toxic levels in her body and relationships. She also had an Emotional Expression Channel (checking the ILR and repeating **Step 10**) of Personal Invasion on all levels (emotional, physical, sexual, and spiritual), expressing subconscious emotional patterns of the behavior "fear of change" (Emotion #10 from the Water element/**Step 11**).

These subconscious emotional reactions were both tied to the holding pattern **(Step 12)**, with a limiting belief in the light body (energy) of her third chakra (solar plexus). Ultimately, Colleen's body and life were manifesting what I call *spiritual myopia* (nearsightedness)—a limiting belief causing her to see herself and the world around her through a lens of helplessness and fear of change **(Step 11)**. Every time this part of Colleen was triggered by any one of her senses, her subconscious inner voice of "helpless" and "fear of change" would play the tape of the third chakra: "I'm not enough; I'm not good enough; if only I were more."

This limiting belief began when Colleen was three years old (original occurrence/**Step 12**). At that time, she didn't have the ability to express: "I'm choosing to have my heart beat with joy!" Even more than this, her environment didn't have the conscious ability to model or teach Colleen that she was powerful beyond measure; her power came from within (power of the third chakra) because those around her didn't realize that for themselves, and people are only able to teach what they know.

This is how the Gift of the Spirit Protection Reflex (SPR), otherwise known as an *imprint,* began **(Step 6)**, and it culminated in the symptoms and stress of challenges with the menstrual cycle and the desire for more—in this case, a relationship. By bridging the gap with The LifeLine Technique and Infinite Love & Gratitude, Colleen could now reclaim her Divine Feminine power and break the misperception that was stemming from when she was three years of age. As we closed the assemblage point **(Step 13)**, walked in place **(Step 14)**, and checked to see if there was any more resistance to Infinite Love & Gratitude associated with the portal **(Step 15)**, I could see the change in Colleen's eyes and hear it in her voice.

Within two months of the first session, Colleen began to authentically attract into her life what she desired . . . her heart beat with joy, and she experienced pain-free menstrual cycles. More important, she developed an authentic, reciprocal, and intimate relationship with *herself,* which has allowed her to enjoy dating. Colleen says her passion and love of life have been reignited, and she loves the amazing journey that she's on![2]

When we all reach the point that we recognize the importance of acknowledging, accepting, honoring, embracing, and celebrating the Divine Feminine in ourselves, as well as in others, I believe our planet will experience a very deep and profound shift, and the healing of Mother Earth's "hot flashes" (global warming) will begin.

The Mind Holding Pattern: Healing Limiting Beliefs

Subconscious emotional patterns of reaction primarily and progressively develop from conception to puberty. The genesis of these programs is our parents, siblings, other relatives, teachers, doctors, religious leaders, government authorities, and such because of the influence and perceived power they have over our lives and environment. These hand-me-down beliefs are transmitted from generation to generation, teacher to student, doctor to patient, politician to the people, and religious leader to followers of a particular faith. During this time, every belief, value, and experience is downloaded as energetic information that becomes the driving force and fuel for all aspects of a person's perception. As a result, one's perception is very predictable on a certain level, and on another is unique to each individual.

In his book *The Biology of Belief,* Bruce Lipton describes the process in this way:

> The subconscious mind is strictly a stimulus-response playback device. . . .The subconscious works only in the "now." Consequently, programmed misperceptions in our subconscious mind are not "monitored" and will habitually engage us in inappropriate and limiting behaviors.[3]

The activation of subconscious limiting beliefs has an impact on every area of a person's life. Lipton's research has been instrumental in helping bridge the gap between the human genetic potential and limiting beliefs. Lipton, a cellular biologist, discovered that people's DNA forms as a result of their perception of their environment. It wasn't DNA that predicted the outcome of someone's heredity disposition, he noted, but rather the way a person's field is filtered through the conscious and subconscious minds that is the real driving force in the development of chromosomal combinations.[4] The Mind Holding Pattern of The LifeLine Technique Flow Chart is associated with the subconscious programming of these limiting beliefs, which are held in the light body of the chakras.

The Unified Field of Light

When light is reflected through water, it refracts—bending and forming a prism. The prism comprises the seven specific colors that both macrocosmically make up the rainbow and microcosmically make up your light body. This prism is known as a *chakra,* which literally means "wheel" or "disk." Although our awareness of the number of chakras in the human body and auric field continues to expand as we deepen our understanding of the body's energetic field, in The LifeLine Technique we focus on seven. Each of the colors has a unique capacity and function based upon its wavelength, its speed of movement, or its rate of change. (For detailed information about the specific chakras, see *The Power of Infinite Love & Gratitude,* pages 136–140.) These variable light bodies are where basic *changes* and transformation from life to death, nonphysical to physical, and spirit to body occur.

The essence of each of the chakras is based upon its fundamental potential for change. Physical matter vibrates at slower frequencies and takes longer to change. On the other hand, the nonphysical body vibrates at faster frequencies and takes a shorter time to do so. Even though the human body appears to be solid matter, it's actually a body of light in a constant process of transformation. Therefore, the potential for change exists for our physical body just as it does for our light body.

Each chakra acts as an electromagnetic field attracting and repelling energies based upon their specific polarity. As a result, life can be perceived through the lens of negative or positive experiences. This concept can be very challenging—it's easy to become attached to, and therefore identified by, relationships, jobs, social status, or even symptoms.

Limiting Beliefs Stored in Chakras

Those limiting beliefs that are subconsciously programmed from your environment, parents, teachers, and so on are down-loaded and stored as frequency files within your chakras. When activated through the senses, those beliefs cause the chakras' light to be distorted, affecting your perception, behavior, and physiology.

The journey of a limiting belief in the light body of the chakras will turn on a part of the physical cell called the *sensory protein receptor.* As the name implies, sensory protein receptors are in each of the senses. My view is that they form in response to the energetic conductance of the chakras, acting as antennae that then send signals to a part of the brain called the *hypothalamus.* The hypothalamus balances and regulates many different functions of the brain and body; however, its primary job is to regulate the pituitary gland—the master hormone gland—which produces neuropeptides, the molecules of emotion (identified by Candace Pert, Ph.D.) that form in direct relationship to one's environment. Neuropeptides are messengers that mirror the internal essence of your body with the external environment you call your life. The potential for neuropeptides to reflect both of these environments is based upon the circuit breaker of limiting beliefs. They act like a lock and key, activating and deactivating each and every one of the trillions of cells in your body.

Let me give you an example. All of your life, you've dreamed of becoming a professional singer, performing on stages around the world, including Broadway. In high school, you were subconsciously imprinted with the limiting belief that you didn't have enough talent to sing when your choir director reassigned your solo for the holiday concert to someone else. On a conscious level, you were so angry with the choir director that you pursued your passion anyway "just to prove him wrong." However, you deeply respected his opinion, and the limiting belief about your abilities began to take subconscious root. As you pursued your professional singing career, you experienced chronic bouts of laryngitis and emotional stress, such as performance anxiety, which further perpetuated the limiting belief.

Why did this happen? Let's answer this from the perspective of The LifeLine Technique. Every chakra has a specific power. The fifth is called the *throat chakra,* and its power is the authentic expression of your truth; its color is blue. Every time your senses are triggered by the color blue or some other sensory experience associated on a subconscious level with the original encounter you had with the choir director—a melody or smell—the limiting belief is activated. You're unable to express your passion and truth through singing.

The chronic laryngitis and performance anxiety are the *symptoms representing the gap* between your conscious beliefs in yourself and the subconscious imprint you received in high school. The gap can be bridged by setting an intention with respect to where you're going as if you're already there, and harmonizing with the power of Infinite Love & Gratitude.

Activating the Light of the Chakras

The Mind Holding Pattern section of The LifeLine Technique Flow Chart uses The LifeLine Color Therapy Chakra Glasses. There is a pair for each one of the seven chakras—red, orange, yellow, green, blue, indigo, and violet—used to activate the light body of the particular chakra found to resonate with the limiting belief. The bent-arm muscle-reflex test will immediately go weak when the eyes perceive the specific color associated with the chakra being activated. Pinching one's hair when the glasses are put on deactivates the sensory protein receptor that has formed as a result of the limiting belief. Hair is protein and acts as an anchor to bridge the energy of the chakras to both the physical and behavioral aspects of a person's body and life.

The research of Bruce Lipton demonstrates how this mechanism impacts the genomic expression of DNA.[5] Your DNA produces cells throughout the body to help you adapt to the external environment. For example, people living in extremely cold climates produce chromosomes in their DNA that manufacture more fat cells to help keep the body warm. The bodies of people living in hot climates, on the other hand, form skin cells (darker pigment) that enable them to adjust to prolonged exposure to the sun. So which came first—the chicken or the egg? Belief or biology?

The energy of our environment is filtered through the chakras into the senses via sensory protein receptors. The binary nature of life expresses itself as love or fear, action or reaction. The subtle difference between thriving and surviving is solely based upon a memory resonating as a limiting belief or an imagination filled with infinite possibilities. Your brain and body don't know the difference. However, because the subconscious will always override the conscious, the DNA that constructs the blueprint of who you are biologically and behaviorally resides in the light body of your chakras. Use your imagination and create your life through the power of intention!

Longing to Know Your Truth

The Mind Holding Pattern enables you to follow the timeline backward to the original occurrence when you were first programmed with a limiting belief. Returning to the original occurrence, while remaining in the safety of the present moment, allows the mind and body to experience and examine the limiting belief from the point of view of an *observer*. In fact, you may not even remember a particular event; rather, you'll connect to the feelings or images that are a result of a subconscious limiting belief program. Whatever the case, once they're harmonized, your clarity and vision are transformed. You'll no longer need the subconscious, protective emotional lens. Based upon the intentions you set for yourself, there's an infinite universe awaiting your discovery far beyond the walls of limitation.

With Infinite Love & Gratitude, the genetic patterns associated with limiting beliefs are harmonized, providing you with the capacity to *choose* in the moment. Until you experience it, it's almost hard to fathom—but what once caused you to think, feel, and act with pain, fear, and stress will no longer bind you to the past. Instead, your capacity to love yourself unconditionally will be activated and unleashed; you can now begin to fulfill your life's destiny.

The Body Holding Pattern:
The Limitless Possibilities for Regeneration

One of the most amazing aspects of the subconscious mind is nonjudgment. Your body responds automatically to environmental stimuli based on primal reflexes. The formation of these reflexes begins at conception and becomes the basis of every function, ranging from your physiology to your psychology.

Every species has at its core a set of primal reflexes that are the foundation of the physical life and perpetuation of that species. For example, suckling is a primal reflex that humans have at birth. The suckling reflex is activated immediately when a nipple, bottle, or finger is placed in the newborn's mouth. There's no judgment or "thinking" about the process; it automatically begins and will continue as long as it's activated.

The same nonjudgment occurs later in life. The subconscious mind activates a physiological reflex that is identical whether, for example, you're running a race for a great cause or running away from a fire. It simply reacts by increasing your heart rate, respiration, and muscle tone.

The Body Holding Pattern represents a similar state of passive reaction. Subconscious emotions are expressed behaviorally and physically, which eventually leads to chronic imbalance, also known as a chronic maladaptive stress response, in the body. Degeneration can occur in any aspect—elements, cells, organs, glands, pathogens, senses, or systems. It's this subconscious, chronic maladaptive stress response that's the emotional root of degenerative processes such as heart disease, cancer, and osteoporosis.

This is your journey—whatever Body Holding Pattern you may be experiencing is the place where you can begin to untie the bow of the gift. The LifeLine Technique Body Holding Pattern is similar to an energetic form of surgery, without the scars and hospital stay. The physical regeneration I've witnessed in my clients as a result surpasses anything I learned in school or anything that exists in current textbooks. Sometimes the changes are instantaneous; other times there's a process of healing that needs to be supported with the Five Basics for Optimal Health (Step 16), or what we refer to as the *Essential Acts of Self-Love.*

The Spirit Holding Pattern: Helping Your Spirit Know Peace

As much as we love to multitask, the mind can only focus on one thing at a time. Take a moment and attempt to think about several things—a project at work, what you're going to have for dinner, and what you're planning to do over the coming weekend. You'll find that your mind will switch pictures to focus on one primary scene at a time. During a traumatic or dramatic experience, however, the nervous system becomes vigilant and reactive as a means to adapt and survive.

The Spirit Holding Pattern represents subconscious attractor fields that draw dramatic or traumatic experiences and hold them in the electromagnetic field of the body. On a quantum level, the trauma and drama behave like a wave or a particle:

— A dramatic or traumatic **wave** pattern impacts every aspect of life, ranging from health to relationships. When activated, a wave of trauma causes dissociation between the spirit and the will. The choices you make directly impact the way the spirit moves through your body or how *you* move through life. When the spirit and will are dissociated in the subconscious mind, the spirit can't be sustained, motivated, or potentiated.

— A dramatic or traumatic **particle** represents specific experiences that result in the lack of Present Time Consciousness (PTC). These subconscious holding patterns create a protective field through dissociation and/or distraction. When a particle of trauma is activated, there's dissociation between the mind and body. Without a clear connection between them, the potential for healing, complete regeneration, and wholeness is limited.

The Spirit Holding Pattern creates a protective field through dissociation and/or distraction. Whether the subconscious pattern of protection is a wave or a particle, its purpose is to inhibit the processing of a perceived experience of trauma. The limbic brain is responsible for learning, regulating healing, and protection. This system controls the sleep cycles called *REM,* which stands for "rapid eye movement." It occurs when the mind, body, and spirit integrate short-term memory into long-term memory. This memory is involved in how cells interact, relationships grow, and information is processed.

Once the subconscious patterns of protection are discovered, integrated, and harmonized, your body and life begin to heal on both cellular and emotional levels.

As a result of tens of thousands of LifeLine sessions I've performed, I have come to recognize and understand the protective mechanism set in place in the electromagnetic field as a result of trauma. This mechanism then extends to the nervous system as a chronic maladaptive stress response, resulting in difficulty falling or staying asleep. Depending upon which direction a person's eyes are looking at the moment of perceived trauma, the experience becomes locked in every cell in the body and relationship in life as a pattern of dissociation or disconnection.

Experiences are downloaded from the spirit's electromagnetic field into specific files of the limbic brain. These files are never processed from short-term memory into long-term memory on a physical and emotional level so that higher centers of the brain can access them for both creative and logical input. As a result, we get stuck in time and space and are unable to grow, learn, and heal.

Every time a person looks in the specific direction associated with the moment of the original trauma, a glitch occurs. Instead of a smooth-running vessel, we have hiccups in the body's function or in different aspects of life. When activated, a Spirit Holding

Pattern is akin to traveling at a high speed on the freeway when someone suddenly reaches from the backseat and puts the car's gear into park. The results can be catastrophic.

The nervous system is locked out from processing and integrating the emotional experience through the four stages of REM. The trauma stays lodged in the holding pattern of the subconscious mind, manifesting in the electromagnetic field of the mind, body, and spirit. Just as a magnet attracts and repels depending upon its polarity, the trauma does the same. This process perpetuates traumatic relationships—between the cells of the body, with people . . . even the relationship you have with yourself!

Let me give you an example. Laura Pawuk is a Certified LifeLine Practitioner and a board-certified music therapist who specializes in hospice care. She shared with me an experience she had with one of her clients:

> Annie is a kind and funny 95-year-young woman who is bed bound. Her daughter and son-in-law care for her in their home; their family is supported by a hospice team for end-of-life needs. Typically an easygoing, lighthearted person, Annie unexpectedly became combative during bath time. When Jenny, the hospice home-health aide, attempted to gently bathe her, she would become very angry and afraid. Once, when Jenny turned her over, Annie even hit her.
>
> Annie's daughter asked me to conduct a LifeLine session during one of our scheduled music-therapy sessions to address this challenge. Her daughter served as the surrogate and helped me create the portal by engaging her mother in a brief conversation.
>
> "Do you remember the last time that Jenny was here to bathe you?" her daughter asked.
>
> Annie nodded her head yes and gazed deeply into her daughter's eyes. Despite the diagnosis of dementia, Annie understood. Her daughter continued to recount the bathing challenges that Annie experienced while I conducted the LifeLine session.

Muscle-reflex testing revealed that Annie's subconscious was reacting with spiritual (in all aspects of her body and life) imbalance, causing her to disconnect from her will—her power to make conscious choices. The story began to make sense: Annie felt out of control during her bath.

The emotions associated with bathing included those of the Water element, such as fear, paralyzed will, and the inability to make choices. The experience was being held in the spirit/ electromagnetic field as a traumatic wave, where conscious love doesn't exist. I synthetically re-created the eye pattern where the trauma was being held. The direction of the eyes—from far to near—meant that the fear and paralyzed will were associated with current experiences that her mind was unable to download during sleep at night. This motion also represented Annie's perception of Jenny as she approached her to turn her over or bathe her.

As a way to prepare for the bath with Jenny, I encouraged Annie's daughter to acknowledge her mother's feelings, create opportunities for her to make choices, and remind her that she has control.

To conclude the LifeLine session, Annie's daughter acknowledged the feelings of fear and lack of control her mother had been experiencing. She affirmed that she would be in control at the next bath time and would be given the chance to choose which body parts were to be washed, especially those that were the least threatening, such as her hands and arms. Despite the dementia, Annie appeared to understand. She nodded, spoke quietly, and intently listened to her daughter.

I reinforced Annie's feelings and power to choose by allowing her to be in charge of the music-therapy session. I invited her to select which songs to listen to; which instruments to play; and whether or not she wanted to sing, listen, or play. Annie effortlessly engaged in choice making, music making, and moving to music. She picked the songs "Beer Barrel Polka," "Edelweiss," and "Side by Side," which led to a discussion about the unconditional love and support that she would continue to receive no matter how challenging her life becomes.

Prior to Annie's next bath, her daughter reminded her that she would choose which body part she wanted washed and that she would be in control.

When Jenny arrived, Annie's affect expressed that she wanted to say no. But when she looked at her daughter, she consented. In fact, she chose to have her hair and belly washed, but not her feet. Annie remained completely calm while being turned; and her expression was very bright, energetic, and engaged throughout the process.

Her daughter felt great relief that her mother would no longer be triggered by bath time. She also felt a sense of empowerment because her "prebath talk" was supportive to her mother's ability to remain in control.

In the months since the treatment, Annie has rarely expressed any irritation about being bathed. To the delight of her daughter, at nearly every bath Annie has consistently remained easygoing, calm, and in control.[6]

When it comes to REM patterns, there are a total of up to four stages that need to be harmonized. If the brain doesn't go through the four stages of REM, then healing doesn't occur on a physical and emotional level. Healing, learning, and changing require REM patterns. Without them, people begin to break down, have poor memory, and rigidly follow the same way of living their lives. Re-creating synthetic eye patterns enables traumatic or dramatic experiences to be processed.

Harmonizing the Spirit Holding Pattern frees and reconnects the will and spirit and the mind and body, making it possible to achieve the intention set in the beginning of the session with The LifeLine Technique (Step 2).

Ultimately, the traumas and dramas of your life are conversations letting you know that at one point your spirit didn't have the tools, strategies, or support to process emotions. Observing your relationships, you may find that there are Spirit Holding Patterns in your subconscious mind. Harmonizing these patterns will change your life in ways you could only imagine.

In the next chapter, you'll learn about the assemblage point—the location of the original disconnection from your spirit, from your infinite truth.

⊕⊕⊕ ⊕⊕⊕

CHAPTER 25

Step 13: Assembling the Spirit for Peace

"In the West we identify with the side of matter, which is by nature finite. The shaman identifies with the side of energy, which is by nature infinite."
— Alberto Villoldo, Ph.D.

At the point of conception, one sperm joins together with one egg to create one cell; in other words, 1 + 1 = 1. It's the evolutionary road that each of us travels on the journey to become the 50-trillion-plus-cell organism called a human being, making us all biological phenomena that defy the laws of mathematics.

From the conception of human life to the birth of divine inspiration, there is a gap between what we know to be true and what is *actually possible.* As a consequence, we judge our life, health, relationships, finances, and so on based on those perceived limitations.

Outside of indigenous cultures where shamans teach that possibilities are only limited by perception,[1] few people have been courageous enough to consciously challenge the gap. The first person who comes to mind is one of my favorite composers—the prolific Ludwig van Beethoven. Beethoven wrote his greatest compositions while he was progressively losing his hearing. In a moment of total conviction, he bridged the gap between what he knew to be true (going deaf) and what was actually possible (writing the extraordinary symphonies being performed in his mind). The late Helen Keller—with the assistance of her determined and devoted teacher, Anne Sullivan—bridged the gap of being blind, deaf, and mute to become one of the greatest writers and humanitarians of the 20th century. Mahatma Gandhi changed the destiny of two nations by bridging the gap between what he knew to be true (the necessity of ending human-rights violations) and what was possible (independence for India). The list is endless and operates on both the macro- and microcosmic levels.

While speaking on the Ocean of Gratitude Cruise in 2008, Rev. Michael Bernard Beckwith noted that what occurs at any given moment depends on our perspective:

> We don't see because we have eyes . . . we have eyes because we can see. We don't hear because we have ears . . . we have ears because we can hear. We don't feel because we have a heart . . . we have a heart because we can feel.[2]

Step 13: The Assemblage Point of The LifeLine Technique Flow Chart provides the means for challenging, transforming, and bridging the gap created by our limited conscious view of symptoms and stress. Specifically, it represents the location within the microcosmic orbit (the circulating flow of energy along the midline of the body) where incongruence exists between the attractor fields of the conscious and subconscious minds. This incongruence manifests as the potential for change to occur (what's actually possible).

It's easier said than done, because when your heart begins to beat with a subconscious emotion like fear, the conscious mind is unable to discern whether the fear is current, past, or imagined. The larger the gap in consciousness, the less awareness you'll have of the potential for personal power and transformation.

During Step 13, your intention is to bridge the gap between the conscious and subconscious minds. Restoring the assemblage point with Infinite Love & Gratitude harmonizes the subconscious emotions that limit perception of the truth (the spirit is pure love) and awakens you to what's possible (Step 2).

ASSEMBLAGE POINT

The Microcosmic Orbit

Keep in mind that whenever you perceive your life or your body as heavy, tight, constricting, compressing, or out of control, it's a direct signal that the light of your spirit is receiving directions from the subconscious mind—from a part of you whose awareness is other than the present moment, the now. Think of symptoms as a spiritual feedback mechanism and the associated pain, fear, and stress as the means for awakening the potential within you to consciously choose love. Remember, you can't comprehend what you don't know until you *know* it.

The microcosmic orbit bends the light of pure love and begins to express itself in physical form. This physical manifestation initially travels along two specific acupuncture meridians called the *Ren Conception Vessel* and the *Du Governing Vessel*. The Ren Conception Vessel runs up the midline of the body from the perineum (the space between the genitals and the anus) to the inside of the lower lip, and is said to reflect your inner experience, how you actually feel. The Du Governing Vessel reflects incoming energy and the visible result of your use of this energy in life. It runs from the tip of the coccyx (tailbone) up the midline of the spine over your head and ends at the inner part of the upper lip.

I recently had a profound experience involving a client and the microcosmic orbit. Helena is a musical angel of light who lives in

Europe. She is studying to become a psychologist, but she currently refers to herself as a "psychotherapist of life." We worked together for more than a year via telephone before we actually met in person at a LifeLine Technique Training Program. Here is her story:

> I was born with a cleft lip, a congenital deformity. A cleft is a fissure or opening—a gap. It's a nonunion of the body's natural structures that form before birth. As a newborn, I received surgery to correct it, which left a prominent scar.
>
> As a child, I smiled a lot. People always commented on my smile. Although I played with other children, I never felt connected to them. I was numb on the inside. As I got older, to mask those feelings of isolation and numbness, I immersed myself in school—I have two bachelor's degrees (one in psychology and the other in social anthropology and cultural sociology), and have trained in Reiki and Soul Coaching.
>
> Over the past 14 years, I searched for ways to release the numbness that I knew was preventing me from opening my heart. One of my passions was playing the cello and singing. However, I always felt self-conscious about performing and expressing my creativity in front of others. I'd heard that the cello is known for its incredible range of emotional expression, capable of penetrating the heart. I now realize I subconsciously chose the cello as a means to penetrate my own heart and get in touch with my feelings. I also sought the assistance of a psychotherapist; bodyworker; homeopath; craniosacral therapist; Chinese medical doctor; clairvoyant advisor; and other people who worked in the area of mind, body, and spirit. But it wasn't until I began my work with Darren that I felt myself able to uproot the numbness and begin to transform my life.
>
> The astrological intuitive Robert Ohotto referred me to Darren, suggesting that I contact him as a means of "bridging the gap" (a term Darren uses in all of our sessions) of what he described as the "trauma consciousness" dominating my life. I e-mailed Darren to inquire whether he conducted phone sessions. He responded promptly, saying he would be honored to work with me.

Soon my behavior began to astonish me, as well as the people who knew me best. I found myself spontaneously singing, smiling, and laughing. My spirit was rising, and the dark clouds of numbness began to part. I actually was having a hard time believing it, but I could *feel*.

I decided to accelerate my healing process by attending The LifeLine Technique Training Program five-day intensive in Hahndorf, South Australia. On the last day, I asked Darren if I could sing a song to the group. I was simultaneously confident and nervous—it was a very funny *feeling*. But I didn't let it stop me. I sang a Brazilian song about bridges, because its theme encapsulated The LifeLine Technique—no matter how wide the gap, there's always a bridge. As I sang, I experienced my heart bursting with love in response to Darren's tears of joy.

As everyone packed up at the end of the training, Darren made time to conduct a LifeLine session with me. My intention was to "be in my full power, happy, and joyful." While I don't remember all of the details or all of the subconscious emotions, some of the things Darren said during the session brought back memories of the reading I had with Robert Ohotto the year before. There were three layers of limiting beliefs that began when the cleft lip was surgically repaired as an infant. The second layer of limiting beliefs went back to the point of conception. The third was in a past life in the year 1652 when I was nine years old and in a traumatic environment. Darren explained that the Ren Conception and Du Governing vessels meet at the lip. The symptom of the cleft lip is a fissure or a gap formed as the result of the gap that existed when I spiritually incarnated into this lifetime. The subconscious patterns—the gap—dominating my life were complete misperceptions that were ready to be transformed with Infinite Love & Gratitude.

I can say unequivocally, the performance anxiety is gone. Even the facial scar tissue from the surgery for the cleft lip is softened and a lot less visible. I am ready to live my best life, regardless of my life's experiences. I now choose to be joyful and happy![3]

A break is created between the Ren Conception Vessel and the Du Governing Vessel every time there is a gap between the conscious and subconscious minds, resulting in the assemblage point—the vortex or epicenter—of the human energy field's vibrating atomic and quantum particles. It can be said that the assemblage point is the lens through which we experience life. We know from the manifestation of symptoms that when that lens is askew, nothing appears clearly in present-time light. But when it is bridged, the horizon is filled with hope, joy, happiness, and peace.

⊕⊕⊕ ⊕⊕⊕

CHAPTER 26

Step 14: Integration of the Mind, Body, and Spirit

*"Change your allegiance from fear to love,
and love will sustain you wherever you walk."*

— Alan Cohen

"I'm walking; I'm breathing; I'm moving and releasing. I'm walking and breathing, and now I can move on!" Certified LifeLine Practitioner and my dear friend Debra Hale, whose story you read in Chapter 20, created this catchy song for her clients to sing during Step 14 of the LifeLine session with the goal of integrating the body, mind, and spirit.

When you're walking in place while breathing deeply, you activate a core primal mechanism of healing and wholeness for efficient integration of the body, mind, and spirit. It's associated with the cross-crawl pattern that pediatrician William Sears says is an essential part of human development between ages six to ten months.[1]

Cross-crawl activates the part of the brain called the corpus callosum, the major tract of nerve fibers that connects the right and left hemispheres. It can be thought of as a *bridge* between the two hemispheres—as the highway in the brain through which information passes from one half to the other. This bridge is what enables a person to integrate both creative and logical thoughts, feelings, and actions. Accessing this creative and logical bridge stimulates momentum and an opportunity for peace to occur. Without delving deeper into the study of neurology, "walking and deeply breathing" activates what is called the cross-crawl pattern.

The cross-crawl pattern is a necessary component in learning how to walk. A number of developmental challenges have been noted in children who don't effectively develop this pattern. Cross-crawl dysfunction is associated with the following:

- Learning disabilities
- Lack of coordination
- Inability to read or reading difficulty
- No concept of balance
- Clumsiness
- Stuttering
- Seeing or saying words backward
- Dropping objects
- Tripping frequently

As a result of being born with severely bowed legs, I spent the first year of my life in casts. Consequently, I didn't develop the cross-crawl pattern. In school, I had many challenges with learning, and I also have memories of it being difficult to learn to skip. It seemed as if I couldn't get my body to do what I wanted it to do. After I awakened to The LifeLine Technique, I was able to heal the symptoms associated with the cross-crawl dysfunction. Even more important, when my son was born with severely bowed legs in 2008, I used sessions with The LifeLine Technique to bridge the generational gap of subconscious emotional patterns that resulted in the symptom of bowed legs in his life. Within three to four months of multiple sessions with The LifeLine Technique, my son's legs were completely straightened out, and he became a champion crawler!

WALK and BREATHE

Walking and breathing at the end of performing a session with The LifeLine Technique teaches the body, mind, and spirit how to integrate as a unified being. Then the process of *feeling* begins. Remember, you have to feel to heal. There is no other way around it. When you do open up to those feelings, a whole new world opens up to *you,* as noted in the following e-mail I received from Maryse, a client and now a Certified LifeLine Practitioner who lives in Delaware:

> Thank you for triggering my *feeling* journey. I would like to share an experience with you. I recently ran a session on myself connected with my childhood/life issues with my mother. The next night I dreamed a sequence of symbolic scenes: At first I was in the same toxic/hate environment of my younger years. Then there was an earthquake. I fell off the roof where I was hiding. My cell phone was permanently lost. Then a moving van pulled up in my driveway. Finally, an RV pulled up to pick me up. The funny thing is that I woke up in the middle of the dream to go to the bathroom. I went back to sleep and it continued.
>
> A lot has shifted since then. For the first time in almost 59 years, I *feel* compassion for my mother. The pain and many negative emotions seem to have disappeared. I feel free! I have plenty more to clear and keep working at it! But so much *feels* different since this significant chapter. Every baby step I take toward my recovery is as exhilarating as any huge one I witness in someone else. So once again, thank you so very much for the magical science you have discovered and the Love you spread! Everyone you reach will never be the same. We are blessed to have found your teachings and our own healing tools! Life is so beautiful, and so are you![2]

Whether you're running a session on yourself or on someone else, you always walk in place and deeply breathe with intention after the assemblage point. Because we're all microcosms of the macrocosm of the universe, when you conduct a LifeLine session on yourself or on someone else, the ripple of energy impacts all of humanity. Imagine . . . the whole world healing and feeling as one!

The Connection Between Symptoms and Space Travel

During a flight between Melbourne and Sydney, Australia, where I was conducting The LifeLine Technique Training Program, I sat next to an astrophysicist. I've always been fascinated by space travel and began to ask him questions. During the course of our conversation, I could see the interconnection—the microcosm within the macrocosm—between symptoms and space travel.

The space shuttle has two huge booster rockets, he told me, responsible for getting the shuttle off the ground. The fuel in these tanks is nitrogen based; its combination is so powerful that it propels the shuttle at "warp speed" into the infinite universe. However, not only is nitrogen a nonsustainable fuel, it's also a greenhouse gas that adds to pollution and global warming. The boosters are discarded as soon as they've fulfilled their purpose. Once orbiting in space, a steam engine of sorts utilizes water as a sustainable fuel for the completion of the shuttle's flight.

You share a similar process—your life experiences are often powered by toxic, nonsustainable fuel. Addictive behavior; physical illness; and internalization of the subconscious emotions of anger, fear, low self-esteem, sadness, and vulnerability are potential catalysts for the launch of your life journey. However, just as the space shuttle lets go of the boosters that launched it into orbit, once you're awakened to the true cause of pain, fear, and suffering, it's time to let go of what is no longer serving you. Infinite Love & Gratitude is the sustainable energy necessary to empower your spirit to move through life and allow it to move through *you* with grace and ease.

When you're walking and breathing during Step 14 of The LifeLine Technique Flow Chart, you're letting go of the boosters that got you off the ground, and a new set of engines is now fueling your orbit. You're traveling with intention (Step 2) and are ready to "move on"!

⊕⊕⊕ ⊕⊕⊕

CHAPTER 27

Step 15: Is There Any More Resistance?

"Resistance always shows up in the form of your thoughts. Watch for thoughts that convey your inability to think of yourself in genius terms . . . thoughts of doubts about your abilities . . ."

— Dr. Wayne W. Dyer

In *Step 15: The ILR* of The LifeLine Technique Flow Chart, the Infinite Love Resistance (ILR) indicator muscle is used to evaluate whether there's any resistance to manifesting your intention. In other words, you're asking if the subconscious emotional pattern has been fully harmonized and transformed—has the gap been bridged? When there's no more resistance, change naturally begins to occur on all levels.

I refer to the ILR indicator muscle as the "Love Gun." This hand mode reveals the truth of your consciousness by detecting in Step 15 whether the dialogue with your subconscious mind is completed. In other words, in this step you're seeking to determine whether you're completely present in this moment or if there's a part of you that's continuing to react from another time and space (the original occurrence or event when the Spirit Protection Reflex was activated).

The ILR indicator muscle gives you a clear reading through the "lock out" or "give way" response. As a result of its evaluation of resistance, you can easily harmonize gaps of consciousness, to unleash the self-healing and thriving capacity of your body and life.

Conducting a LifeLine session is analogous to changing the filter on an air or water purifier. As soon as you do, the air or water feels and tastes better and has a completely different impact on the health of the body. What appears to be poisonous or toxic in a person's body or life (symptoms or stress) is ultimately the signal that it's time to change the filter. Once all resistance to Infinite Love & Gratitude is harmonized, you're able to more readily choose love over fear.

ILR STRONG
Back to top:
Recreate the portal

ILR WEAK Finished

There Are No Accidents

When my oldest daughter, Joya, was ten months, my wife went away for a weekend to attend a Nikken conference in Memphis. It was a great opportunity for Sarit to have some time to rest and to learn more about Nikken's products, which we believe help facilitate a healthy lifestyle. That Friday night, I put Joya to bed and turned on cable television in search of a movie. I watched

Hotel Rwanda, a film about the genocide of more than a million members of the minority Tutsi tribe over the course of 100 days by the majority and ruling Hutu tribe in Rwanda. It was a very intense and graphic film; I was deeply shaken and dismayed by the extent of the horror and the senselessness of the attacks.

After breakfast the next day, Joya and I went outside. I placed her in the stroller to walk down to the end of our driveway to retrieve the mail. I was looking at her when I put my hand in the mailbox. Suddenly, I felt excruciating pain, but I had no idea what was going on. I looked at my arm and screamed in terror with the realization that at least 20 bees were swarming there. I yanked my arm out of the mailbox and shook off the bees. I grabbed Joya from the stroller and ran to the house. As I ran, I repeatedly said to myself, "Infinite Love & Gratitude."

By the time we were safely inside, my forearm had swollen to twice its normal size. I placed Joya in a Pack 'n Play and ran into the kitchen. I immediately took about 15 sprays of the Spagyric Botanical Metal (you'll learn more about Spagyric Botanicals in the next chapter) to boost my immune system, and drank three tablespoons of the Nikken product Jade GreenZymes mixed in PiMag water (specially filtered water to enhance cellular absorption) to alkalize my body. After taking the supplements, I conducted a "LifeLine First Aid" session on myself, which lasted about 20 minutes.

When I got to Step 11, the subconscious emotion that came up was "hatred" (#10 of the Wood element). My immediate thought was how much I hated the bees—my reaction was to go back to the mailbox and kill them. Then I had a flash of the film *Hotel Rwanda.* I realized that I was in shock and filled with horror about the Hutus' massacre of the Tutsis; I could relate to the hatred of Hutus for Tutsis. The twin realizations allowed me to feel compassion for the Hutus and Tutsis, and myself and the bees.

When I got to *Step 12: Holding Pattern,* the session went to a limiting belief tied to the fifth chakra—the throat chakra—which represented no voice, no choice, and no ability to express myself.

This limiting belief was associated with a time in my life when I had experienced verbal abuse. I felt full of rage, which was deeply buried. I didn't have the ability to express my needs, and I perceived that there was no one in my environment who was willing or able to meet them.

Looking at the history of the Hutus and Tutsis, the conflict was between perceived "haves" and "have-nots" who had no voice, no choice, and no ability to express themselves. Watching *Hotel Rwanda* and getting stung by the bees activated subconscious emotional patterns of reaction. Harmonizing and releasing the subconscious emotions with Infinite Love & Gratitude, I found that the swelling of my arm was all but gone by the end of the session. Within two hours, there were only a few red spots left on my forearm.

I almost went through the rest of the day without telling anyone, but then realized that what had happened was miraculous. I called my friend Tom and recounted the incident.

"If I didn't know the truth of The LifeLine Technique, I wouldn't believe you," Tom said.

The journey of your mind can take you to the most amazing places. Places that may seem "unbelievable." Know right now that the power necessary for you to shine and heal already exists within you.

Feeling the Shift

Using the ILR indicator muscle will help you recognize if there are any other aspects of the mind's filter in need of spiritual "cleansing." In Step 15, if the ILR indicator muscle "locks out," there's still resistance to Infinite Love & Gratitude, and you must harmonize another layer of the subconscious mind (re-create the portal and begin at the top of the Flow Chart). If the ILR indicator muscle "gives way," there is no resistance to manifesting your intention. You've successfully changed the filter and are ready to move on to *Step 16: The Five Basics for Optimal Health.* The ILR is always used with focused intention (PTC in the moment).

The most common reaction people have at the end of a session with The LifeLine Technique is the feeling of a shift; they feel "lighter." The charge—the physical sensations or pain associated with the original symptom or stress—is usually gone or markedly diminished. More important, they begin to see and recognize the light that exists within them. Sometimes they're laughing in recognition, or weeping with joy because they *feel* changed. The first thing I notice is their eyes—the window of the soul—which are brighter! The furrowed brow of stress is not only erased, but the attending darkness is gone. Their skin looks brighter and smoother!

⊕⊕⊕ ⊕⊕⊕

CHAPTER 28

Step 16: The Tools for Living an Optimal Life

*"If you hear a voice within you say aloud, 'You cannot paint,'
then by all means paint, and that voice will be silenced."*

— Vincent van Gogh

Life is a wonderful adventure filled with moments of the highest of highs and the lowest of lows. This unpredictable journey provides the contrast of a full spectrum of feelings and behaviors that have the potential to shift in a nanosecond. Expressing yourself authentically along the journey is a healthy way of discovering your truest nature.

A child, for example, can quickly go from a moment of laughter and silliness to crying and having a full-blown temper tantrum. The same exists as you observe the weather . . . cool and breezy in the morning, transitioning to overcast in the afternoon; rain heading into evening; and right before the sun sets, a rainbow filling the sky. Observing this natural process of change is a key component to living intentionally, on purpose, and in your power.

The ultimate expression of owning your power is living from your truth. The challenge with this is that we now know that *we never perceive the truth; rather, we only perceive what we believe.* As a result, thoughts, feelings, and behaviors are elicited that cause you to make choices for your health and happiness that don't always have those things in mind; they have in mind the health and happiness for a part of you that is still living from a subconscious-mind perspective. This is why making lasting and sustainable change is a journey rather than a destination. Embracing life as a teacher and opportunity to appreciate the full spectrum of oneself on a deeper level is in and of itself an act of self-love.

Love is the one thing that heals everything, and as a result, the mere act of doing your best activates a healing process for the relationship you have with yourself and your body. Life is a miracle; and the fact that you're an organism that's innately built to monitor, react, and repair itself is fundamentally divine. Understand and appreciate that your choices aren't really what matters . . . it's more the awareness of making them from *love* versus fear that transforms them into divine acts of healing and wholeness. This is a key evolutionary mechanism on both an individual and collective level. You're a unique, beautiful, and purposeful expression of the singular love intelligence of the universe. Choosing from this perspective alone will forever change your life.

The Journey to Rediscover Yourself

There's no one way to live your life consciously . . . anything and everything is possible. Conscious choice requires that you do your best to perceive yourself and the world you've attracted through the senses of acceptance, forgiveness, compassion, and gratitude. This is a much-easier-said-than-done process, as it will require you to face aspects of yourself that many times will create a perception of shame, guilt, and regret. However, rather than these feelings and behaviors representing that you're a bad person, wrong, or broken, in reality they signify the power you now possess to live a life of authenticity and truth.

You're on a journey to rediscovering yourself as you observe your thoughts, feelings, and behaviors as acts of self-love. Do your best to let go and surrender to the possibilities rather than being defined by perceived disabilities. Any thought pattern or behavioral protocol that is rigid in its requirements for living a healthy and full life will at some time reach its limit to carry you to the destiny of your soul.

I personally love to eat delicious food and drink yummy wine. Making choices based on your heart rather than from your head is one of the most liberating and healthy ways of living life to the fullest. Yes, it's okay to eat sugar *every once in a while.* Even more important than avoiding sugar is embracing yourself and the choices you make with love. The LifeLine Technique is a complete system of healing and wholeness that enables you to live from love . . . and love living!

There is an array of different resources you can choose from to live a healthy and happy life. I'm providing you with the best information that I know of and that I'm personally utilizing in my own life. If it feels right, begin to implement these changes. Observe how you feel and take it one step at a time. Your choices impact both your body and behavior; thus the road to inner peace is in actuality the road to world peace. You'll observe the ripple in your family, work, and community.

The Stages of Transformation

There are three stages of transformation on your journey to inner peace:

1. Detoxification
2. Regeneration
3. Thriving

Transformation occurs as a result of bridging the gap between the conscious and subconscious minds. The three stages of transformation are directed at detoxifying the mind, regenerating the mind, and having a thriving mind. Your body and life will naturally follow once your mind begins this process.

Detoxify the Body, Mind, and Spirit

To support the detoxification and regeneration process, I highly recommend products from Dr. Tom Bayne and PureBalance Botanicals. Tom is a highly regarded and internationally renowned expert in functional nutrition and detoxification. He has developed a cutting-edge system of nutritional products to support the physical, emotional, and spiritual body during the three phases of transformation. You can find detailed information at **www .purebalancebotanicals.com**.

Another product I'm excited to share with you is called Just Like Sugar. It's a revolutionary natural sweetener that's made from chicory root (dietary fiber), calcium, vitamin C, and natural flavors from the peel of an orange. It's truly a phenomenal product that is a safe alternative for people whose bodies are speaking to them with diabetes, and it's fantastic for bowel health due to the chicory root. And if that weren't enough, it also tastes great! It can be used for baking as well, and the producers of Just Like Sugar have creatively used it to make many more wonderful products. Check out their Website at: **www.justlikesugarinc.com**.

When it comes down to living an optimally healthy life, the choices you make will either be supportive or destructive. The simple recognition that a choice exists can make all the difference.

Lifestyle Is the Key!

Check Water, Food, Rest, Exercise, Own Your Power

In her book *The Power Is Within You,* Louise L. Hay wrote that "the point of power is always in the present moment."[1] To make the most of the present moment, a healthy lifestyle is an integral component of your journey toward well-being and wholeness. I refer to the healthy-lifestyle components of The LifeLine Technique philosophy, science, and quantum technology as the *Five Basics for Optimal Health.* It's important to make sure that you maintain the proper quantity, quality, and frequency of:

- Water
- Food
- Rest
- Exercise
- Owning your power

More than optimal health, however, the Five Basics are *essential acts of self-love.* Each of these was previously explained in depth in *The Power of Infinite Love & Gratitude.* However, since the writing of that book, I've learned so much more and now have new important information that I want to share. Let's begin with water.

Tool #1: Water—Water Is Life!

Water is the most crucial, nonnegotiable component of optimal health. After all, you can live for extended periods without food, *but not without water.* Why is it so essential?

- Your entire body is 75 percent water.
- Your blood is 82 percent water.

- Your lungs are 90 percent water.
- Your brain is 90 percent water.

In fact, water plays a role in every function of your body, from regulating temperature and cushioning joints to bringing oxygen to cells and removing waste, yet so many people are dehydrated! The levels are alarming.

In October of 2008, *The New York Times* reported a steep rise in the incidence of kidney stones, once a chronic disease that only struck people who were at least 50, in children as young as five or six![2] This disturbing statistic speaks to the crisis state of how our nation is treating children—both their physical and emotional well-being are at risk. From an allopathic perspective, kidney stones are the by-product of too much salt and crisis levels of dehydration. But on an energetic/emotional level, the kidneys are the storehouse of toxins, and too many children have to wrestle with toxic and poisonous levels of fear because the people in their environment don't have the tools or strategies to process their own anxiety and panic. If ever our children and the world needed a lifeline, the time is now!

One of the little-known facts about the importance of water is that it greatly contributes to our ability to process emotions.

In his book *The Shape of Love,* Masaru Emoto wrote: "In a world of water, I don't believe there is such a thing as total despair because water circulates. Water can pass from one form to another and finally come back to its beauty. So, too, can we humans."[3]

Emotions, e-motions, are energy in motion. Water conducts electricity. Without water, the body can't maintain its basic functions, including manufacturing enough energy to process emotions. Take a moment and connect to a stressful situation in your life. If your body is dehydrated, you'll feel this stress as a stinging, burning, or twinge in some area. That's because there's not enough water to conduct the electrical charge that this situation is creating.

In my practice as a holistic physician at The Way to Optimal Health, too often I notice symptoms of dehydration in clients who come to me for the first time. While the answer may seem as simple as "Drink more water," it goes well beyond that. Heather Fougnier is a Certified LifeLine Practitioner whose practice is as mobile as her Internet and telephone connection. She has clients around the world. This experience she shared, which was first published in my monthly newsletter, *The Line,* helps demonstrate the importance of hydration:

> Kevin came in to see me for a LifeLine Technique session. He had been diagnosed with chronic fatigue and was experiencing symptoms of exhaustion, dehydration, and abdominal pain.
>
> I asked Kevin what he loved to do, and I realized that he was disconnected from his passion. As a consequence, he felt stuck and depressed. An airline pilot for almost 30 years, Kevin was feeling bored in his job and in his life. He yearned for something more—more meaning, more excitement. Instead of *living,* he felt like he was *going through the motions* of life. But he was afraid to leave his safe, well-paying job for what he *really* wanted to do . . . travel writing.
>
> Using The LifeLine Technique, I found that Kevin experienced the emotion of low self-esteem at five years old, when his parents got divorced. Because the five-year-old part of him did not have the tools and ability to deal with what was happening at the time, his subconscious mind (which operates under the survival mechanism of fight or flight) stepped in to protect him.
>
> After five sessions of The LifeLine Technique, Kevin was able to reconnect to his will and release the subconscious pattern of low self-esteem. He consciously reconnected to his passion, and he began to take action in pursuing his dream as a travel writer. Today, just one year later, he is doing what he loves.
>
> Kevin is no longer experiencing chronic fatigue, abdominal pain, or dehydration. Connecting to that five-year-old part of him and *releasing the subconscious, hidden emotion* of low self-esteem allowed him to transform his life.[4]

We learn from Kevin's experience that even when you drink plenty of high-quality water, the body won't use it until the subconscious emotional patterns that are inhibiting the flow of energy are harmonized. The LifeLine Technique helped free Kevin's body to heal and his life to transform.

⊕ ⊕ ⊕

The next essential act of self-love is food. Are you eating the emotions you should be expressing?

Tool #2: Food—Understanding the Body's Ecology

When you think about the concept of "eating healthy," what comes to mind? For a lot of people, it means going on a diet. But more and more evidence is showing that diets don't work, and in fact, they often create a vicious cycle of yo-yo weight loss and gain. On top of that, going on a diet is often all about calories and not about how to truly nourish your body. So, where do you begin when you want to start a healthy eating program?

Since the standard American diet (SAD) consists largely of high-sugar and processed foods, the concept of "nourishing foods" has been lost. In fact, many people are experiencing the subconscious emotional patterns of reaction as symptoms of poor digestive health, such as gas, bloating, indigestion, yeast infection, constipation, and abdominal pain. While using The LifeLine Technique to transform subconscious suppressed emotions, the most important component of healing is taking personal responsibility; the quantity, quality, and frequency of what you eat is critical to your health. No matter what symptoms you may experience—and even if you perceive yourself to be in good health—focusing on a healthy eating plan is key for feeling your best.

Support Your Body

Over the years, I have had the privilege of studying many systems of health and healing, and the one that I've recently found to best complement and support The LifeLine Technique is the Body Ecology Diet, created by Donna Gates. I was first introduced to this eating plan by Heather Fougnier, a certified Body Ecologist, while she was studying to become a Certified LifeLine Practitioner. I will never forget how good I felt after the lunch Heather prepared of fish; salad; roasted, sea, and cultured vegetables; and a heavenly dessert called halvah. After lunch, I felt completely satisfied—light and energized.

According to Donna, the inner workings of your digestive tract can be thought of as your "inner ecosystem." When I asked her to describe this, she said, "Just like the earth has ecosystems full of organisms responsible for harmony and balance, our bodies follow suit."[5]

Donna and I both teach that good digestive health is fundamental for feeling your best. On both a mind and body level, your digestive system breaks down and extracts the nutrients your body needs to heal, regenerate, and thrive. Most people have gotten off track with nutrition, as it's become largely about *convenience.* Body Ecology actually teaches us to reconnect with nature and with traditional, whole foods as a way of living.

Donna often says, "While we may be living longer today, we're not necessarily living better. In fact, our ancestors were often more hardy and energetic than we are today."[6]

So while we know our subconscious minds and emotions play a primary role in our best health, food, as Donna teaches, plays a vital role as well.

Feeding Your Emotional and Physical Health

As Donna and I began to study one another's work, we realized that Body Ecology and The LifeLine Technique offer an unparalleled combination for health. The LifeLine Technique helps a person heal both body and life through transforming subconscious emotions, while the Body Ecology program creates optimal conditions in the body for healing to occur.

I've been encouraging my clients to follow the Body Ecology system (**www.bodyecology.com**), and they're experiencing tremendous results; the feedback has been extremely positive. This program helps improve every-one's quality of life, and it enhances the body's ability to reverse the aging process. Imagine that—reversing the aging process with *food!* Want to gain 20 or 30 more years of youthful vitality? Body Ecology is the key!

Organic Does Matter

Still doing your best to decide whether organic is better? Here is some recent information about the science and politics of food production:

- Seventy percent of the antibiotics produced are being fed to livestock.

- A study in *The Journal of Infectious Diseases* reported that people who ate conventional chicken became resistant to strong antibiotics.

- The *Journal of Environmental Quality* found that greenhouse corn, lettuce, and potatoes were grown on soil that contained hog manure with a commonly used veterinary antibiotic added.[7]

If at all possible, eat grass-fed meats; free-range/antibiotic-free chicken; wild-raised fish; and locally grown, organic produce. Is it more expensive? Most times, yes. But your health and that of your family are priceless. Organic is more than worth the investment. According to the International Federation of Organic Agriculture Movements (IFOAM), the first principle of organic farming states that "organic agriculture should sustain and enhance the health of soil, plant, animal, human and planet as one and indivisible."[8] Furthermore:

> This principle points out that the health of individuals and communities cannot be separated from the health of ecosystems—healthy soils produce healthy crops that foster the health of animals and people.
>
> Health is the wholeness and integrity of living systems. It is not simply the absence of illness, but the maintenance of physical, mental, social and ecological well-being. Immunity, resilience and regeneration are key characteristics of health.[9]

Eating organic foods also allows us to develop, cultivate, and maintain a peaceful relationship with our planet, Mother Earth.

Tool #3: Rest—Restoring Balance with Sleep

High on the list of symptoms that new clients frequently discuss with me is insomnia (the inability to sleep) or restlessness (the inability to sleep through the night). Typically, they all have several lifestyle issues in common: emotional overload or high levels of stress; poor bowel habits; consuming too much caffeine; and eating processed foods high in cane sugar, high-fructose corn syrup, white flour, and white rice.

Many have also used doctor-prescribed sleeping pills, causing a drowsy effect, which then leads them to consume even more caffeine in order to feel awake during the day. It usually becomes a painful and vicious cycle whose root, we have discovered through sessions with The LifeLine Technique, has many subconscious emotional patterns of reaction.

Sleep deprivation affects the body's immune system. It can speed up the aging process and the onset of metabolic or hormonal imbalances. As a matter of fact, recent studies have determined that sleep deprivation may be one of the major contributing factors in the increase of type 2 diabetes.[10] Well-known effects of lack of sleep include irritability, blurred vision, slurring of speech, short-term-memory lapses, anxiety, panic attacks, inability to concentrate, and hallucinations.

What's most clear is that there's a direct correlation between the quality of your health and the quality of your sleep. To rest is to restore your body, mind, and spirit. The act of sleeping not only allows your body to heal, but it also enables your mind to process and integrate your life experiences. How well you rest is also impacted by whether you drink enough water, eat healthy foods, exercise daily, and own your power.

Steps for Getting a Good Night's Rest

This is very important—prepare for rest the way you prepare for the rest of your day:

- Establish a set time for going to bed.

- Turn off the TV at least 30 minutes before your planned bedtime.

- Spend 15 to 30 minutes winding down by making the time to be quiet, meditate, read, journal, or listen to soft music.

- Perform deep-breathing exercises to facilitate relaxation. (You can find several in *The Power of Infinite Love & Gratitude,* pages 190–193.)

- Take a hot bath or shower or sit in a sauna before bed.

- Reserve your bed for sleeping, rather than using it as an alternative site for working, watching TV, or studying.

- I recommend that my clients use a sleep system with magnetic and far-infrared technology to enhance deeper states of REM and to balance the body's thermostat.

How Crucial Is Rest?

Western medicine would call Marcia a "medical miracle." However, as she learned, in addition to releasing subconscious emotional patterns of reaction, lifestyle plays an integral role in helping the body heal itself:

> I started seeing Dr. Weissman in 2006 after being diagnosed by my medical doctor with Crohn's disease, which is a very painful inflammatory-bowel process. I wasn't sure about what he was doing when he performed The LifeLine Technique and said the words, "Infinite Love & Gratitude." However, I left after every session feeling as if the shift in my life was profound. He showed me how I had disconnected from my ability to love myself unconditionally. In addition to the sessions, I adhered to the Five Basics of Optimal Health, especially the principles of food and rest. Today, my body is no longer "speaking to me" with Crohn's, which the medical doctor said was incurable![11]

Sleep is an essential tool to increase the potential of the body's natural healing capacity. Making sure you receive quality rest and relaxation is one of the most significant steps you can take to reduce the stress of modern living and create inner peace and balance. When you rest is when you restore!

Tool #4: Exercise—Making Time to Move and Play

More than 20 years ago, researchers examining the evolution of humans determined that our bodies are *hardwired* for movement. Among their findings was the conclusion that physical activity contributed to the evolution of the brain by prompting the nervous system to prepare for an onslaught of new information.[12] Think about it—if movement is integral to the optimal function of the brain, what happens when we're *not* moving? I believe it means we're actually limiting our ability to achieve our highest potential.

We already know the benefits of exercise—increasing energy levels, relieving stress, improving sleep—and it can have a major impact on reversing disease processes. However, have you ever considered exercise as an opportunity just to have fun?

The Importance of Play

Many of us think that "play" is only for children. However, Stuart Brown, a psychiatrist who has spent decades researching this issue, has found that playing is a survival skill and biological necessity for shaping and sharpening the brain.[13] Most of us suffer from a "play deficit," and Dr. Brown says it has serious consequences.

In several studies reported in *Scientific American Mind,* researchers found that unstructured play (play for no other reason than to have fun) is crucial to the social, emotional, and cognitive development of children.[14] They recommend engaging in activities in which there are no time pressures or expected outcomes, using your hands to create something, or joining other people for "purposeless" social activities. When adults play, the studies found, they are less likely to experience anxiety or burnout.[15]

Making Time to Play

I used to have my own struggles with creating time for play and exercise: with a thriving practice, growing training program, speaking engagements, and a family that includes three young children, I had a hard time getting to the gym. To honor my commitment to maintaining balance with the Five Basics for Optimal Health, I had to get serious about personal fitness in order to overcome the challenge of being crunched for time.

During a session with The LifeLine Technique I conducted on myself, I awakened to the need to connect with the joy and fun of exercising, and that became the motivation for choosing the workout program that evolved.

My fun exercise? I play tennis, swim or run outside with my children whenever we get a chance, and work out once a week with a trainer who inspires me and encourages me to laugh as she's pushing me to bring out my best!

The late George Sheehan, who was the editor of *Runner's World*, wrote: "Play opens up our inner world and allows our subconscious to percolate through to understanding." When you play, Sheehan noted, you unlock emotion, understanding, and creativity.[16]

Three Tips to Fully Enjoy the Benefits of Exercise

1. Visualize yourself moving—before you actually do it.
2. Be in the moment—feel each moment.
3. Observe how much fun you're having.

Take a moment and imagine all the ways you can combine exercise and fun with your friends or family—walking on the beach, taking a hike, or riding your bike. Children are more inclined to model the behavior they observe: when you engage in a consistent exercise program, you teach them the value of self-care. You can use The LifeLine Technique to connect to the subconscious joy of moving your body.

Set the intention, such as "moving through life with joy," and then *imagine yourself doing just that—*feel it, see it, touch it, taste it, and hear it. The session will allow you to get in touch with the subconscious patterns inhibiting you from experiencing the joy of moving. Once those patterns are transformed, your life will begin to open to the infinite possibilities of discovering and *creating* joy and inner peace!

Tool #5: Owning Your Power and Living a Quantum Life

To own your power is to step into *your* light and acknowledge the "unborn possibility" that you, and only you, have the potential to give birth to.[17] It's embracing every aspect of your life with passion, purpose, and courage . . . *knowing* that every day, in every way, each experience that you encounter represents the *possibility* to be so much more.

To embrace possibilities, we must open our hearts to change. In her award-winning book *Waking the Global Heart,* author, teacher, and spiritual healer Anodea Judith, Ph.D., wrote:

> To *come of age in the heart* is to enter a rite of passage that transforms ego-centered self-interest into an embodied expression of love. Guilt, fear, or manipulation will never produce lasting evolutionary change, *but what is inspired by love is fueled* by natural willingness, even excitement, to serve a higher purpose. . . . To curse the world is to separate from it. To thank your fate is to move through the lessons more quickly.[18]

Imagine having the courage to "move through" life with Infinite Love & Gratitude, to have tenacity and persistence as the driving force of your life. As I wrote earlier, it would be unrealistic to expect to live pain free. Owning your power allows you to see the possibilities waiting to be born within the pain. Notes Emmett

Miller, M.D., pioneer of mind-body medicine and the co-convener of the groundbreaking California State Task Force on Self-Esteem, it makes a *huge* difference to *choose to live* with the attitude that *sees the value* of thorny bushes bearing roses, rather than complaining that some rosebushes are full of thorns.[19]

Make Proactive Choices

Since the publication of *The Power of Infinite Love & Gratitude,* I have continued *my* evolutionary journey of understanding how important it is to recognize that "owning your power" is a *proactive* process. Proactive means we make conscious choices, rather than allowing ourselves to revert to old habits. I realized that my clients needed additional tools and strategies in order to fully embrace and *live* the results of sessions with The LifeLine Technique. I refer to this new "toolbox" as *Living a Quantum Life.*

The core philosophy of Living a Quantum Life is the belief that we are *co-creators* of our evolutionary journey. When we shed the "identity" of pain, fear, shame, guilt, or suffering, we let go of the old identity previously misperceived to be at the core of our being. We are, like the snake in Native American medicine or the shaman of other indigenous cultures, shedding the old skin. We undergo a transmutation process, a metamorphosis, bringing forth our new, *quantum* self. The snake doesn't long for its old skin the way our human consciousness longs for the past. The snake releases everything it has outgrown and moves forward, without judgment. In Chinese culture, the snake also symbolizes wisdom and beauty. When we live a quantum life, we are wisdom; we are beauty. As we arise to observe and participate in our ever-evolving journey, we're able to *be* love.

Taking Action to Live a Quantum Life

How do you live a quantum life? I believe there are five steps. In the science and art of numerology, the number 5 signifies being open to love; living with compassion; embracing freedom; needing constant change; and striving to find answers to the many questions that life poses, not just for ourselves but also for all of humanity. To live a quantum life, it's imperative to do the following:

1. **Live with vision.** All great leaders throughout history have had a clear vision of a truth that resonated deep within their hearts. This vision became the catalyst that set into motion a new way of thinking, feeling, and being. All great leaders, as a result, maintain their clarity of vision regardless of opposition or perceived capabilities. To live with vision means to take the time to silence the mind so that you can *see* and embrace *your* truth. Activate the power of the sixth sense—intuition—and trust it to guide you. Many people experience their intuitive vision through *different* senses, including the eyes, ears, and skin. The most important thing is recognizing that listening to, trusting, and acting on your intuitive vision is an art; and like any other endeavor or discipline, it requires commitment to develop.

2. **Live with hope.** Hope is a natural consequence of having clear vision. Its birth rises from darkness, fueled with the vision of promise. At its core, hope allows you to believe in what's possible . . . if one person can, we all can. Feel this emotion in your heart. It's the *feeling* that *imagines, sees,* and *knows* at every juncture of the journey. Hope is the reflection of truth, wholeness, divinity, and oneness. "Roll up your sleeves" and let's work together. In a world where many see hopelessness as being as normal as the rising sun, begin today to challenge yourself to harvest and sow seeds of hope.

3. **Live with passion.** Passion is the energy of your will. It's what empowers you to take action, transforming hope into possibilities. The question is, what's *your* passion? What *moves* you to get out of bed every day? What makes your heart flutter when you think about it? Do you go to work *just to get paid?* Do you want to know how to live with passion? Answer this question: What would you be doing at this very moment in your life if you knew with absolute certainty that you couldn't fail? Allow yourself to honestly and authentically answer this question—from the deepest part of your heart—acknowledging the ever-unfolding inner voice of Infinite Love & Gratitude.

Sometimes voices of fear and doubt take over. Do you know those voices? "I don't have any money." "I don't have enough education." "I have too many kids." "I'm too old." "No one would ever pay me to do this. . . ." Living with passion is not about *doing;* it's about *being.* It's not how you get paid, but rather how you live. The feminist scholar Gloria Anzaldúa once wrote: "The possibilities are numerous once we decide to act and not react."[20] Decide to act and live with passion. A moment of passion will transform a breaking point into one that is inspirational.

4. **Live with discipline.** Discipline distinguishes mastery from mediocrity—mastery that comes from spending time engaged in the journey, rather than sprinting the 50-yard dash. Living with discipline means being willing to change—to alter old patterns of how you consciously choose to respond to your life. With discipline, you can gain insight and wisdom into your *true* nature. When you accept the inevitability of change, you choose healthier options for yourself.[21] Rather than being a rigid set of rules, living with discipline is based on *conscious* acts of self-love. It's loving yourself enough to choose between the pleasures of the moment and the possibilities of an infinite spirit.

5. **Live with gratitude.** These days, almost everyone is talking about gratitude. But what does it really mean? I was inspired by

a quote I recently read in a tiny but powerful book on gratitude written on behalf of the LifeLesson Foundation by Lenore Skomal:

> Our role is to accept what happens to us and to do what we can with the possibilities that life offers us. Acceptance is the key to this. If we can stop trying to figure out what we did wrong to warrant the problems that we face, and just accept it as part of what happens while living on this planet, we can find immense freedom. Life is what it is. And if we can reach unconditional acceptance of that, then the door to true gratitude will open.[22]

To live with gratitude is to accept, embrace, forgive, learn, and live with the *knowing that life itself is the greatest of all gifts.*

You've Taken a Giant Step

The 1-2-3 PLAN of The LifeLine Technique is an organic, ever-evolving, quantum-healing technology. Every time I have a session with a client, or teach The LifeLine Technique Training Program, I discover new avenues to help people experience their power for self-love and inner peace. I am in awe of the process, humbled by its magnitude, and beyond grateful to be able to share it with the world.

✦✦✦ ✦✦✦

CHAPTER 29

We Are All One

"When the power of love overcomes the love of power,
the world will know peace."

— attributed to Jimi Hendrix

With all of the pronouncements that have been made in this book about the "power of Infinite Love & Gratitude" and "your mind's journey to inner peace," you're likely wondering if The LifeLine Technique has *really* been put to the test. The experience I'm about to share with you is the moment I understood the true potential of light to emerge from darkness—the *single moment* that helped me understand that there is *always* so much more. For me, ground zero for this awakening was Kinglake, Australia.

The fires during Australia's drought-stricken summer of 2009 were fanned by gale-force winds and fueled by a heat wave of more than 117 degrees Fahrenheit (47 degrees Celsius). Located 32 miles northeast of Melbourne, Kinglake was among the hardest-hit towns—500 homes were destroyed in a town of only 1,400; close to 40 people, too many of them children, were confirmed dead.

I was on a mission to Kinglake, joined by Certified LifeLine Practitioners Madge Bares, Susan Isoe-Schneider, and Mary Beth Shannon. Our mission was to spend two days offering sessions with The LifeLine Technique to people whose hope and lives were consumed by the fire. Our friend Diane McMann Mathews of Adelaide, South Australia, arranged for her friends David and Enrica to drive us to the relief center.

Days before we departed, we heard media reports that there wasn't much left of Kinglake. What was once home to a world-renowned national park, a famous winery, wildflowers, wallabies, kangaroos, platypuses, and kookaburras was reported to be filled with soot and ash. As we rode in the car to the relief center, looking at the skeletons of trees, fragments of houses, and blistered car shells littering the landscape of what had been the favorite haven for the urban dwellers of Melbourne, these earlier reports seemed like an understatement. Previously vibrant and thriving neighborhoods were now pockmarked by charred remnants of people's lives—scorched gnome statues, blackened bird feeders, twisted metal bike frames, and crumbled brick chimneys. The acrid air was thick and noxious—a choking stew of burned wood, burned flesh, and burned metal. The areas where families used to gather and children used to play were now blocked off by blue and white striped police tape. That was where the incinerated bodies were found, we later learned.

I was struck speechless by the silence. No bird sounds, no animal screeches, no rustling of leaves. The stillness was palpable, visceral; it scratched my skin. This scorched earth filled with singed carcasses of trees, skeletons of animals, and soot piled high like mounds of gray snow felt like a war zone. Having conducted LifeLine sessions with quite a few veterans returning home from armed conflict, I understood how and why they disconnected from the consciousness of love. It's painful beyond words to even allow yourself to *fathom* the searing pain of so much loss. My heart was cauterized by the overload of my senses. I felt a wall go up that allowed me to see, but I knew I was in shock. I was aware of being numb.

The wall around my heart made it impossible for me, a conscious observer of my body and my life, to feel what I was experiencing. The protective mechanism was so strong that even The LifeLine session I conducted on myself to unleash the waves of sorrow being suppressed couldn't yet penetrate it. Like a soldier on the front lines, I was at full attention and ready to be of service. But like some of the veterans I had worked with, my heart had moved into the "untouchable" zone.

A Lighthouse Amid the Darkness

There were people lined up outside of the relief center waiting for us to arrive when our car pulled in to the driveway. As we all got out, I told Madge, Susan, and Mary Beth that we would conduct sessions with The LifeLine Technique as usual—follow the 1-2-3 PLAN and bridge the gap.

"Keep it simple," I encouraged them, "and let the rest unfold." What that unfolding turned out to be was a lesson of great significance for all.

The relief center was located in the home of Rhonda McGibney, an angel who had been providing free holistic-health services for anyone in need of help and support in Kinglake West and Flowerdale. Those seeking assistance could find volunteer massage therapists, acupuncturists, home-cooked food, and lots of hugs. Although Rhonda's home had been encircled by the fire and remnants of complete devastation remained, her house had been spared. It became a lighthouse amid the darkness her neighbors were experiencing.

The first day we worked on 30 people in the individual rooms that Rhonda set up for us to conduct sessions. From kids to adults, everyone was in a state of shock and confusion. They had lost parents, children, friends, neighbors, pets, businesses, and their hope for the future. They were unsure where to go or what to do next.

As a LifeLine Practitioner, I was still able to acknowledge their experiences, their emotions, in the face of knowing that a part of me was walled off. At the same time, I could help them interpret their own perceptions of this experience. What's so outrageous is that the part of us that perceives trauma isn't who we are now, but rather *who we were at other times in our lives*. These parts become activated to help us let go of what was once an effective way of processing emotion but is no longer valuable for staying present in the current experience. This is where the pain, fear, and stress come into play.

As I've written throughout this book, symptoms, whether subtle or extreme, are a conversation—a dialogue stemming from the subconscious mind. As soon as we harmonized the subconscious emotional patterns of reaction at the root of the distress felt by the people impacted by the fire, their experience (the symptom) immediately changed. They no longer saw the fire as the "end" of their lives, but rather as a part of their journey.

What's even more fascinating is that one of the Five Elements consistently showed during the sessions I conducted with The LifeLine Technique—Water. Kinglake had been in a drought for more than eight years, but while we were there, it began to rain. You may view this as happenstance, but the quantum perspective of the universe is that there is no separation between us and nature; what goes on inside also goes on outside, and vice versa. Once the energy of the Water meridian was opened for the people we worked on to feel and release, it had a ripple effect on their community, as well as their environment.

Reconnecting to My Spirit

The night after the first sessions, we went back to our hotel. I had intense nightmares. Via e-mail, my close friend and colleague Jeri Love encouraged me to write about my experience. Jeri is a Certified LifeLine Practitioner, a writer, and a writing coach. She explained that the act of writing, like The LifeLine Technique, allows you to step back from a challenging or traumatic situation and *observe* it; the observation allows you to move through it from the perspective of a *witness,* rather than as a participant.

The next morning I woke up and wrote about my experience and e-mailed it to Jeri. After sending that e-mail, I cried for two hours. It felt so good to cry; I could feel the wall of my heart coming down. Now *I was feeling.* I didn't even know that I'd been holding back those tears. Here's the catch: because the function of the subconscious mind is protection, it wasn't going to release those feelings until it was clear that I had the conscious tools, strategies, and support to choose love regardless of circumstances.

On the second day at Kinglake, there was a perceptible difference in the sessions I conducted. I held a deeper space of compassion; I could feel. I cried with just about every one of my clients. I reconnected to my spirit.

I have *always* been confident deep in my heart that The LifeLine Technique holds the potential to help any and every *willing* person transcend painful, scary, and stressful experiences of life. The mission to Kinglake awakened me to an even greater promise—whether it's tragedy, disaster, or war, The LifeLine Technique transforms devastating experiences into those that are both valuable and meaningful. To see terror and hopelessness *visibly* shift into calm and peace, even when there was no immediate tangible change in the external circumstances, reaffirms my heart's calling.

The mind's journey to inner peace is discovered by awakening to the secret code of your mind. With deep compassion and a brave heart, each one of us now has the power to take the next step.

The 16 Steps to Inner Peace

Imagine the implications and applications: broken hearts, broken families, high school dropouts, kids on drugs, neighborhoods ravaged by violence, domestic violence, college-campus shootings, tyrannical governments, prisoner education, political corruption, health-care crises, pandemic viruses, cancer, economic instability, terrorism, genocide, combat zones, border wars . . . fear, fear, fear. Imagine every area of your own life and the world you live in transcended and transformed. Peace begins with you.

Begin by asking yourself this question: "How can I be any more powerful than I already am?" Buried deep within you is a light ready, willing, and able to shine. Your journey inward reveals the value and meaning of every painful, scary, and stressful experience. Choose to step into the perceived darkness and grab the LifeLine. This, in and of itself, is the most powerful act of self-love. A life of peace, hope, courage, and faith is yours to live. Keep shining! The simple truth is that *we are all One,* and the step you take for yourself holds the infinite power and potential for generations to come. Imagine that!

⊕⊕⊕ ⊕⊕⊕

Endnotes

Introduction

1. Chopra, Deepak. *Peace Is the Way* (New York: Three Rivers, 2005).

2. Lipton, Bruce. *The Biology of Belief* (Carlsbad, CA: Hay House, 2008).

3. Printed with the permission of client.

Part I: Breaking the Code of Your Mind

Chapter 1: Love's Universal Healing Power

1. Emoto, Masaru. *Messages from Water* (Tokyo: Hado Publishing, 1999).

2. *Ibid.*

3. Photos from the book *The Message from Water* by Masaru Emoto. Reprinted with permission of I.H.M. Co., Ltd., authorization number: ihm0604030576.

4. Printed with the permission of client.

5. Printed with the permission of Certified LifeLine Practitioner Mary Vogel, **mavogel40@comcast.net**, and her client's mother.

6. Braden, Gregg. *Secrets of the Lost Mode of Prayer* (Carlsbad, CA: Hay House, 2006).

Chapter 2: The Science of Love

1. Collinge, William. *Subtle Energy* (New York: Warner Books, 1998).
2. www.heartmath.org
3. *Ibid.*
4. *Ibid.*
5. *Ibid.*
6. Braden, Gregg. *The Spontaneous Healing of Belief* (Carlsbad, CA: Hay House, 2008).
7. Hay, Louise L. *You Can Heal Your Life* (Carlsbad, CA: Hay House, 1999).
8. Printed with permission.
9. Printed with permission.

Chapter 3: What Do You Choose?

1. Ocean of Gratitude Cruise, www.oceanofgratitude.com.
2. Reprinted with the permission of Shawn Gallaway, www.shawngallaway.com.
3. Eden, Donna. *Energy Medicine* (New York: Tarcher/Penguin, 2008).
4. Printed with permission.
5. The Academy of Psychosomatic Medicine, *Psychosomatics* 45: 448–449, October 2004.
6. Printed with the permission of client's mother.

Chapter 4: The Measure of Healing

1. Printed with the permission of client.
2. Weissman, Darren. *The Power of Infinite Love & Gratitude* (Carlsbad, CA: Hay House, 2007).
3. www.thinkexist.com
4. Printed with the permission of client.
5. Printed with the permission of client.
6. Weissman, Darren. *The Power of Infinite Love & Gratitude* (Carlsbad, CA: Hay House, 2007).
7. Weissman, Darren. "Water: The Fusion of Science and Spirit," in Masaru Emoto, *The Healing Power of Water* (Carlsbad, CA: Hay House, 2007).

Chapter 5: Preparing the Road to Peace

1. Williamson, Marianne. *A Return to Love* (New York: HarperPerennial, 1996).

2. Printed with the permission of Certified LifeLine Practitioner Kally Efros, **www.compactcompass**; her mother, Barbara; and her sister, Kristi.

3. Hawkins, David. *Power vs. Force* (Carlsbad, CA: Hay House, 2002).

Chapter 6: The Path to Peace

1. Graham, Martha. *Blood Memory* (New York: Washington Square Press, 1992).

2. Printed with the permission of Certified LifeLine Practitioner Madge Bares, **http://webmail.infiniteloveandgratitude.com/exchweb/bin/redir.asp?URL=http://www.awakeningintention.com.**

3. Skomal, Lenore. *LifeLessons™: Gratitude* (Kennebunkport, ME: Cider Mills Press, 2006).

4. Jampolsky, Gerald. *Love Is Letting Go of Fear* (Berkeley, CA: Celestial Arts, 1979).

5. Weissman, Darren. *The Power of Infinite Love & Gratitude* (Carlsbad, CA: Hay House, 2007).

Chapter 7: Living in the Now

1. **www.britannica.com**

2. Printed with the permission of client.

3. Hawkins, David. *Power vs. Force* (Carlsbad, CA: Hay House, 2002).

Chapter 8: To Know What We Know

1. Thoreau, Henry David. *Walden; Or, Life in the Woods* (Mineola, NY: Dover, 1995).

2. "The Subconscious Mind: Your Unsung Hero," by Kate Douglas, December 2007, **www.newscientist.com**.

3. Lipton, Bruce. *The Biology of Belief* (Carlsbad, CA: Hay House, 2008).

4. *Ibid.*

5. *Ibid.*

6. *Ibid.*

7. *Ibid.*

8. Printed with the permission of Diane McCann Mathews, **www.beyondtheordinary.net.au**.

9. Printed with the permission of Annie Marosy Kenny.

10. Hay, Louise L., and Friends. *Gratitude: A Way of Life* (Carlsbad, CA: Hay House, 1996).

Part II: Interpreting the Code of Your Mind

Introduction to Part II

1. Hay, Louise L. *You Can Heal Your Life* (Carlsbad, CA: Hay House, 1999).

Chapter 9: Becoming a Master of Dialogue

1. Apatow, Robert. *The Spiritual Art of Dialogue: Mastering Communication for Personal Growth, Relationships, and the Workplace* (Rochester, VT: Inner Traditions, 1998).

2. **www.hsl.virginia.edu/historical/artifacts/antiqua/ hippocrates.cfm**

3. Printed with permission of Certified LifeLine Practitioner Debbie Loshbough, **ilgatlanta@gmail.com**, and client, Paul K.

4. Kendall, Henry and Florence. *Muscles, Testing and Function,* 2nd Edition (New York: Williams and Wilkins, 1971).

5. Hawkins, David. *Power vs. Force* (Carlsbad, CA: Hay House, 2002).

6. *Ibid.*

7. *Ibid.*

Chapter 10: Guidelines for Muscle-Reflex Testing

1. John, James. *The Great Field* (Fulton, CA: Elite Books, 2007).

Chapter 11: The Infinite Love & Gratitude Sequence (ILS)

1. Laskow, Leonard. *Healing with Love,* 2nd Edition (Bloomington, IN: Author's Choice Press, 2008).

2. Emoto, Masaru. *The Miracle of Water* (New York: Atria/Beyond Words, 2007).

3. Hawkins, David. *Power vs. Force* (Carlsbad, CA: Hay House, 2002).

Chapter 13: *Step 1:* The Reconnection—Expanding Your Sense of Oneness

1. McTaggart, Lynne. *The Field,* Updated Edition (New York: HarperCollins, 2008).

2. Braden, Gregg. *The Divine Matrix* (Carlsbad, CA: Hay House, 2007).

3. *Ibid.*

4. For more information about Carol Freeman's work and the Endangered Species Photography Project, check out: **www.inbeautyiwalk.com**.

Chapter 14: *Step 2:* Creating What Is Possible, Now!

1. Weissman, Darren. *The Power of Infinite Love & Gratitude* (Carlsbad, CA: Hay House, 2007).

2. Printed with the permission of client.

3. Chopra, Deepak. *Perfect Health* (New York: Harmony Books, 1991).

4. Braden, Gregg. *The Divine Matrix* (Carlsbad, CA: Hay House, 2007) and *The Spontaneous Healing of Belief* (Carlsbad, CA: Hay House, 2008).

5. Wolf, Fred. *Dr. Quantum's Little Book of Big Ideas* (Needham, MA: Moment Point Press, 2005).

6. Adam. *Intention Heals* (Coquitlam, B.C., Canada: DreamHealer, Inc., 2008).

7. Collinge, William. *Subtle Energy* (New York: Warner Books, 1998).

8. McTaggart, Lynne. *The Intention Experiment* (New York: Free Press, 2007).

9. Laskow, Leonard. *Healing with Love* (Bloomington, IN: Author's Choice Press, 1992).

Chapter 15: *Step 3:* Opening the Doorway to Your Authentic Self

1. Printed with permission of Certified LifeLine Practitioner Gail Keeler, **www.healwithlifeline.com/gail**.

2. Jampolsky, Gerald. *Teach Only Love* (Hillsboro, OR: Beyond Words, 2000).

Chapter 16: *Step 4:* Time to Create Balance

1. Memorex commercial: **http://en.wikipedia.org/wiki/Memorex**

2. The works of Dr. Paul MacLean (Triune Brain Theory), Dr. Joe Dispenza *(Evolve Your Brain),* and Dr. Bruce Lipton *(The Biology of Belief).*

3. Brennan, Barbara. *Hands of Light* (New York: Bantam, 1988).

4. Weissman, Darren. *The Power of Infinite Love & Gratitude* (Carlsbad, CA: Hay House, 2007).

5. Emoto, Masaru. *The Miracle of Water* (New York: Atria/Beyond Words, 2007).

Chapter 17: *Step 5:* Awakening to Your Power

1. Printed with the permission of client.

2. Printed with the permission of Certified LifeLine Practitioner Hayley, **seatofthespirit@gmail.com**.

Chapter 18: *Step 6:* The Gift in Strange Wrapping Paper

1. Truman, Karol. *Feelings Buried Alive Never Die . . .* (Brigham City, UT: Brigham Distributing, 1991).

2. Siegel, Bernie. "Gratitude: A State of Mind," in Louise L. Hay and Friends, *Gratitude: A Way of Life* (Carlsbad, CA: Hay House, 1996).

3. Printed with the permission of client.

Chapter 19: *Step 7:* Change . . . a Natural Part of Life

1. Printed with the permission of Certified LifeLine Practitioner Mary Beth Shannon, **www.JoyfulHealingArts.com**; and Certified LifeLine Practitioner Steve Spencer, **protouchrehab@gmail.com**.

2. Wauters, Ambika. *Life Changes* (Freedom, CA: Crossing Press, 2004).

3. Based on author's study of Chinese medicine and the Five Element Theory.

Chapter 20: *Step 8:* Energy in Motion (E-motion) Stays in Motion

1. Eden, Donna. *Energy Medicine* (New York: Tarcher/Penguin, 2008).

2. Printed with the permission of Certified LifeLine Practitioner Debra Hale, **www.debrashealinghands.com**.

Chapter 21: *Step 9:* Being Creative, in Control, and Whole

1. Connelly, Dianne M. *Traditional Acupuncture and The Law of the Five Elements,* 2nd Edition (Laurel, MD: Tai Sophia Institute, 1994).

Chapter 22: *Step 10:* Expressing Your Truth

1. Jampolsky, Gerald. *Love Is Letting Go of Fear* (Berkeley, CA: Celestial Arts, 1979).

2. Hawkins, David. *Power vs. Force* (Carlsbad, CA: Hay House, 2002).

3. Weissman, Darren. *The Power of Infinite Love & Gratitude* (Carlsbad, CA: Hay House, 2007).

4. *Ibid.*

5. *Ibid.*

6. *Ibid.*

7. *Ibid.*

8. *Ibid.*

9. *Ibid.*

10. *Ibid.*

11. *Ibid.*

12. Tolle, Eckhart. *A New Earth* (New York: Penguin, 2005).

13. *Ibid.*

14. Dispenza, Joe. *Evolve Your Brain* (Deerfield, FL: HCI Books, 2008).

15. Weissman, Darren. *The Power of Infinite Love & Gratitude* (Carlsbad, CA: Hay House, 2007).

16. Printed with the permission of Certified LifeLine Practitioner Kathleen Maxwell, **www.triumph4me.com**.

Chapter 23: *Step 11:* Emotions, the Energy That Moves You

1. Braden, Gregg. *The Divine Matrix* (Carlsbad, CA: Hay House, 2007).

2. Printed with the permission of author's friend David Schiffman.

Chapter 24: *Step 12:* The Key to Healing, Regeneration, and Wholeness

1. Printed with the permission of Certified LifeLine Practitioner Sharon Faw, **swfaw@aol.com**.

2. Printed with the permission of client.

3. Lipton, Bruce. *The Biology of Belief* (Carlsbad, CA: Hay House, 2008).

4. *Ibid.*

5. *Ibid.*

6. Printed with the permission of Annie's daughter and Certified LifeLine Practitioner Laura Pawuk, **laurapawuk@gmail.com**.

Chapter 25: *Step 13:* Assembling the Spirit for Peace

1. Villoldo, Alberto. *Shaman, Healer, Sage* (New York: Harmony Books, 2000).

2. Author's notes.

3. Printed with the permission of client and Robert Ohotto, **www.robertohotto.com**.

Chapter 26: *Step 14:* Integration of Mind, Body, and Spirit

1. **www.babycenter.com/0_developmental-milestones-crawling_6501.bc**

2. Printed with the permission of Certified LifeLine Practitioner Maryse Lavercier, **maryse1129@cs.com**.

Chapter 28: *Step 16:* The Tools for Living an Optimal Life

1. Hay, Louise L. *The Power Is Within You* (Carlsbad, CA: Hay House, 1991).

2. "A Rise in Kidney Stones Is Seen in U.S. Children," by Laurie Tarken. *The New York Times,* October 27, 2008.

3. Emoto, Masaru. *The Shape of Love* (New York: Doubleday, 2007).

4. Printed with the permission of client and Certified LifeLine Practitioner Heather Fougnier, **www.nowradianthealth.com**.

5. Interview between author and Donna Gates, developer of Body Ecology.

6. *Ibid.*

7. **www.mercola.com**

8. IFOAM, **http://www.ifoam.org/about_ifoam/principles/index.html**

9. *Ibid.*

10. "Scientists Finding Out What Losing Sleep Does to a Body," by Rob Stein. *The Washington Post,* October 9, 2005.

11. Printed with the permission of client.

12. Kimiecik, Jay. *The Intrinsic Exerciser* (New York: Mariner Books, 2002).

13. Brown, Stuart. *Play: How It Shapes the Brain, Opens the Imagination, and Invigorates the Soul* (New York: Avery, 2009).

14. "The Serious Need for Play," by Melinda Wenner. *Scientific American Mind,* February 2009.

15. *Ibid.*

16. Kimiecik, Jay. *The Intrinsic Explorer* (New York: Mariner Books, 2002).

17. Holmes, Ernest. *The Science of Mind: A Philosophy, A Faith, A Way of Life* (New York: Tarcher/Putnam, 1998).

18. Judith, Anodea. *Waking the Global Heart: Humanity's Rite of Passage from the Love of Power to the Power of Love* (Fulton, CA: Elite Books, 2006).

19. Miller, Emmett. "Gratitude: A Healing Attitude," in Louise L. Hay and Friends, *Gratitude: A Way of Life* (Carlsbad, CA: Hay House, 1996).

20. Anzaldúa, Gloria. "La Conciencia de la Mestiza: Towards a New Consciousness," in Carole Ruth McCann and Seung-Kyung Kimi, eds., *Feminist Theory Reader: Local and Global Perspectives* (New York: Routledge, 2003).

21. Wauters, Ambika. *Life Changes* (Freedom, CA: Crossing Press, 2004).

22. Skomal, Lenore. *LifeLessons™: Gratitude* (Kennebunkport, ME: Cider Mills Press, 2006).

⊕⊕⊕ ⊕⊕⊕

The LifeLine Technique
Glossary of Terms

Activate: Refers to the process of having our senses triggered by an external stimulus, causing an internal reaction.

Activation pattern: Represents the internal reaction that occurs both biologically and behaviorally. For example, the body's innate response to maintain balance during stress is to increase its heart rate, blood pressure, or blood-sugar metabolism.

Assemblage point: The continuum of energy orbiting the midline of the body, moving along the microcosmic orbit. The assemblage point represents an energetic gap between the conscious and subconscious minds. It's a subconscious point of disconnection. The LifeLine Technique is the conscious point of reconnection.

Biochemical Expression Channel: There are two aspects of the Biochemical Expression Channel—*feeding* and *drainage*. Feeding represents a deficiency of subconscious emotions that need to be *felt*. Drainage represents a poisonous and toxic level of subconscious emotions that need to be *released*.

Body Holding Pattern: The body is a mirror reflection of the energy that feeds its potential. Every thought, action, and reaction is a reflection of the patterns that have subconsciously programmed the body; programming begins the moment the sperm meets the egg. A Body Holding Pattern represents a subconscious chronic maladaptive stress reflex leading to degeneration. Harmonizing the Body Holding Pattern enables the body to be the self-healing and thriving organism it was designed to be.

Bridging the gap: Putting the potential of gratitude into action is the attitude it takes to bridge the gap. The process of discovering the subconscious meaning behind a conscious symptom or stress. Infinite Love & Gratitude is the universal healing frequency to bridge the gap.

Chakras: A Sanskrit word, *chakra* means "wheel" or "disk." Chakras are the energy centers of the body. Each moves with a spinning motion, forming a vortex. It's these vortices that filter the energy of the environment around us and disperse it through the seven chakras of the body. We are light beings. When light contacts water, it refracts and reflects outward as a rainbow. This rainbow configuration is the chakra system. The light body of the chakras is where the frequency of limiting beliefs is held, resulting in a misperception based on both a biological and behavioral level.

Chi: In Chinese medicine, *chi* refers to life force or the energy that travels within the organ meridians. In The LifeLine Technique, chi is emotion, the energy that's moving you.

Circadian Flow: The rhythmic flow of life force. In the Five Element Theory, it refers to the 2-hour period during the 24-hour daily cycle in which each acupuncture meridian functions at its highest peak.

Conscious Body Portal: Represents the subconscious patterns that are creating physical pain or inhibiting it from healing. The Conscious Body Portal uses physical pain—for example, low-back pain, headaches, or stomach pain—as a way into the subconscious mind. Any discomfort in the physical body can be used to bridge the gap between the conscious and subconscious minds.

Conscious Mind Portal: Represents the subconscious patterns that are creating stressful situations in life or inhibiting you from releasing the stress. The Conscious Mind Portal provides awareness of the emotional connection to physical symptoms or stressful experiences in life—for example, addictions, phobias, traumatic memories, panic attacks, and so on. Stressful experiences are a dialogue stemming from the subconscious mind expressing a gap between the conscious and subconscious.

Disease: A state of the physical body where there has been a pathological breakdown of at least 40 percent. When these pathological processes can be observed through diagnostics—such as blood tests, urine tests, and radiographic procedures—a diagnosis can be given to that process. The medical profession treats disease with pharmaceuticals and surgery. Certified LifeLine Practitioners never diagnose, treat, or cure disease. Rather, they bridge the gap between the conscious and subconscious minds.

Dis-ease: *Dis-ease* = without ease. It's your body's and life's way of expressing imbalance.

Emotions: Energy in motion will stay in motion unless met by another force. Emotion is a part of everything and everyone, everywhere and all the time. There is only one emotion, and that is love. Love is infinite, and therefore everything is love expressing itself the best way it knows how. The power of emotions is experienced in our thoughts, feelings, and actions. These emotions are then filtered into our physical bodies and relationships and flow throughout the acupuncture meridians of the mind-body, connecting all parts of a person's physical self and life. Harmonizing subconscious emotional patterns of reaction is the key to healing, wholeness, and transformation.

Expression Channel: The Expression Channel lets you know *why* your body or life is speaking with symptoms and alerts you to the subconscious conversation that's being used to awaken you to owning your power. The Expression Channel is either *emotional* (behavioral), *structural* (physical), or *biochemical* (inability to feel or let go of feelings).

The Five Basics for Optimal Health: The quantity, quality, and frequency of water, food, rest, exercise, and owning your power are essential acts of self-love.

The Five Element Theory: The Five Elements—*Fire, Earth, Metal, Water,* and *Wood*—represent change. They help us appreciate that the natural flow of energy that occurs within nature also occurs within our bodies and relationships.

The Five Steps for Quantum Living: Refers to conscious actions to co-create your life: live with *vision, hope, passion, discipline,* and *gratitude.*

Free will: Will represents choice . . . the freedom to choose regardless of circumstances of race, gender, religion, nationality, education, and so forth. Free will only exists in the conscious mind. Many people do not express their free will due to a fear of change.

Frequency: A measure of electricity distinguished by the units of hertz. The body is electrical. We know this to be true, as we use diagnostic determinants such as an EKG, EEG, or EMG to measure the health of the heart, brain, or muscles. Multiple different frequencies harmonize together to manifest as the physical body. The vibrational frequency of the mind will determine the vibration at which a person's body and life thrive or survive. Infinite Love & Gratitude is a universal healing frequency.

Frequency of disease: A gap between the conscious and subconscious minds leads to corrupt frequencies and stagnation in the mind and body. Stagnation leads to an accumulation of poisonous and toxic emotions in a person's body and life.

Harmonize: Refers to a process to create balance and congruency within and/or between a person's body, mind, or spirit.

Holding Pattern: Refers to the area in which a symptom that's persisting to protect you is being held. The Holding Pattern is either in the *mind* (due to limiting beliefs), the *body* (causing degenerative processes), or in the *spirit* (creating an attractor field of trauma or drama).

Holographic Principle: We live in a quantum universe that is holographic in nature. Each part of the universe is a mirror, bridge, and reflection, where one piece represents the whole. Emotion is the life force and web that connects the holographic universe. The LifeLine Technique uses symptoms to bridge the gap between the conscious and subconscious minds, thereby having a holographic impact on the collective conscious mind of humanity.

ILR: Stands for the *Infinite Love Resistance*. It's the brakes of the vehicle for the subconscious mind. When the ILR "locks out" using the MRT, there's a gap present between the conscious and subconscious minds. Infinite Love & Gratitude bridges all gaps, and as a result causes an ILR indicator muscle to "give way." No resistance means high conductance.

ILS: The ILS represents the *Infinite Love Sequence,* the universal frequency of healing.

Intention: A vision of where you desire to be, created as if you're already there.

Ko: Each of the Five Elements has a relationship with the others. The Ko cycle is the destructive, or controlling, cycle. This represents the subconscious part of oneself that is feeling controlled or out of control.

The LifeLine Law of Transformation and Creation: Emotions transform energy; energy creates movement; movement is change; and change is the essence of life.

The LifeLine Technique: The LifeLine Technique is both an ancient and advanced complete system of healing and wholeness. It's a philosophy, science, and quantum technology that bridges the gap between the conscious and subconscious minds. At the root of every symptom, stress, and disease is a subconscious emotional pattern of reaction. When activated, this pattern of reaction will cause both behavioral and biological stressors. The cornerstone of The LifeLine Technique is the Five Basics for Optimal Health—the quantity, quality, and frequency of water, food, rest, exercise, and owning your power. Anyone who is passionate about taking responsibility for their life and consciously bringing out their best can be trained to be a Certified LifeLine Practitioner. There are currently Certified LifeLine Practitioners throughout the world. The truth is that The LifeLine Technique can't be explained . . . it's an experience.

Luo: The connection between the yin and yang acupuncture meridians of a particular element. The Luo cycle represents the subconscious interdependence of polar opposites and thus a person's ability to be whole.

Maladaptive stress response: A quantum, subtle, acute, or chronic emotional pattern stemming from the subconscious mind. This is the means by which the subconscious mind communicates, expressing symptoms in all of its extremes. As spiritual beings, we are able to maintain a spiritual evolution through the primal expression of a maladaptive reflex. It's designed to foster self-love.

Microcosmic orbit: The circulating flow of energy that follows the Ren and Du acupuncture meridians along the midline of the body. This flow of energy has polarity and attracts and repels life experiences according to the harmony between the conscious and subconscious minds. The chakras represent specific light bodies along the microcosmic orbit that bridge the internal microcosm of the body with the external macrocosm of the universe.

Mind: There is one infinite mind; however, for the purpose of understanding, it's broken down into five parts.
1. *Conscious*—perception and choice
2. *Subconscious*—protection and reaction
3. *Super-conscious*—manifestation of intention
4. *Collective conscious*—the mind of humanity
5. *Collective unconscious*—the mind of God

Passion: Refers to an experience of the heart based upon feelings that fuel a person's will to make choices. Passion is a means to living a spiritual life and awakening to the divine essence of each and every experience. It's not found *in* something, someone, or someplace, but rather is a sustainable fuel that's always present.

Pathology: Pathology is diagnosable disease. For pathology to be present, the body needs to be more than 40 percent broken down.

Power Center: The Power Center is the area of The LifeLine Technique Flow Chart that represents the subconscious mind. Also known as the super-conscious or microcosmic orbit, the Power Center consists of the *mind* (thoughts), *heart* (feelings), and *will* (choice). The Power Center is the soul of a person and represents what power has been sacrificed as a means of protection. Reconnecting to one's soul power (thoughts, feelings, or choice) helps create balance in one's physical body and relationships in life.

Present Time Consciousness (PTC): PTC is the act of staying connected to a moment, regardless of how painful, scary, or stressful an experience is. PTC enables you to acknowledge, honor, and embrace your feelings, stay in tune with your senses and intuition, and live life with compassion and acceptance. By authentically responding to what you're experiencing, you are empowered by PTC to live life with courage, faith, and personal truth.

Shen: Each of the Five Elements has a relationship with the others. The Shen cycle is the creative cycle. This represents a subconscious part of a person who is internalizing, denying, or disconnecting, or who has lost creativity.

Spirit: Spirit is pure love. It represents the body's electromagnetic field. A person's physical self and life begin to change when the spirit is able to flow with grace and ease. A gap between the conscious and subconscious minds causes the spirit of pure love to bend its direct course into the body. The result is an inefficient flow and connection between the mind and body, resulting in symptoms.

Spirit Protection Reflex (SPR): The primary purpose of the subconscious mind is to keep the spirit safe by creating gaps of consciousness. This is called the Spirit Protection Reflex (SPR). Your ability to choose love, create efficient tools, and develop strategies for thriving is directly related to the primary relationships in your life. Parents (especially mothers), siblings, extended family, teachers, religious leaders, doctors, the media, and so on imprint patterns of either love or fear. The SPR is a spiritual feedback mechanism that keeps the spirit safe while simultaneously providing an opportunity to learn to resonate at one's highest vibration while in physical form.

Spiritual feedback mechanism: Analogous to a biofeedback mechanism for the body, the spiritual feedback mechanism is a way to recognize sometimes subtle, and other times extreme, automatic/autonomic patterns of reaction.

Spiritual myopia: The gap between the conscious and subconscious minds acts as a filter or lens of misperception. People are unable to recognize their truth of love and egoically begin to identify themselves as an experience or a physical symptom that is painful, scary, or stressful. This is a mechanism of protection that stays in place until they've strengthened the conscious muscles of seeing and choosing love.

Subconscious emotional pattern of reaction: An imprint pattern based upon a gap between the conscious and subconscious minds. It is associated with an earlier experience during which you didn't have the *conscious* tools, strategies, or support to choose love.

Subconscious mind: Represents what's below the surface. We are unaware of the functions of the subconscious mind, as they are below consciousness. The subconscious mind is in charge of all of the major bodily functions, including heart rate, blood pressure, immunity, hormone balance, sugar metabolism, digestion, and detoxification, just to name a few. It's also where emotions, memories, and beliefs that have not been processed and integrated are stored. The sole (really, *soul*) purpose of the subconscious mind is protection and evolution of the spirit. When a consciousness of other than love is present during a time of perceived trauma, the subconscious mind creates a gap as a means to incubate a part of us until we are ready to choose love. Symptoms and stress are the subconscious mind's way of letting us know that we're now ready to choose love. The subconscious mind is in charge of 90 to 98 percent of our awareness, memory, and function.

Super-conscious: The super-conscious mind is the next evolution for humanity. Once humanity has bridged the gap individually, and thus collectively, we as a collective group will be attracting as a super-conscious field. The possibilities are infinite, as one's only perception from a super-conscious mind is love. Just because people are super-conscious doesn't mean that they don't feel pain, get scared, or experience stress. Rather, they choose love regardless. The super-conscious mind represents the power center on The LifeLine Technique Flow Chart once the conscious and subconscious minds have been bridged. A super-conscious person is able to think, feel, and act with love in any given situation.

Symptoms: Refers to the language that the subconscious mind uses to represent that a gap is present between the conscious and subconscious minds. All symptoms are a conversation, a true dialogue that leads us back to the truth of our nature. Both our bodies and lives speak our minds. We are spiritual beings having a human-being experience where all roads lead to love.

Triad of Health: Represents a person's body and relationships in life that have been reacting with subconscious imbalance. There are four parts to the Triad of Health—*emotional, biochemical, structural,* and *spiritual.* It represents the specific location where an imbalance has occurred, leading to a resistance of flow of emotion.

Yang: The Chinese name given to represent *positive, hollow, white, sky, external, male, active, above, kinetic,* or *fire.* Depending upon the perspective, something may be yang or yin. The yang acupuncture meridians are the outer meridians along the Five Elements.

Yin: The Chinese name given to represent *negative, solid, black, earth, internal, female, passive, below, potential,* or *water.* Depending upon the perspective, something may be yin or yang. The yin acupuncture meridians are the inner meridians along the Five Elements.

⊕⊕⊕ ⊕⊕⊕

Information and Resources

Please visit **www.drdarrenweissman.com** for more information about:

- **One-day trainings offered by specially trained Certified LifeLine Practitioners** (helping you master the skills of muscle-reflex testing and the 1-2-3 PLAN for manifesting your intentions)

- **Becoming a Certified LifeLine Practitioner**

- **Tools to help you learn The LifeLine Technique:**
  — Home-study kits, which include DVDs, CDs, podcasts, and written material
  — *Muscle Reflex Testing* DVD
  — *Conscious Body–Conscious Mind* 6-DVD set
  — The LifeLine Technique Flow Chart audio CD
  — The LifeLine Technique wall and handheld Flow Charts
  — The LifeLine Technique Emotions Chart

- Finding a Certified LifeLine Practitioner in your area

- Joining Dr. Weissman's Weekly *Road to Inner Peace* Healing Circle

- Setting up an appointment at The Way to Optimal Health: 847-714-1531

- Inviting Dr. Weissman to speak at your conference

⊕⊕⊕ ⊕⊕⊕

Index

Acknowledgments

As has been said, "It takes a village to raise a child." There are so many amazing and generous people who made this book possible. However, there's a certain person who stood above the rest, championing, motivating, and inspiring me to shine. This book would not be possible if it weren't for Jeri Love. With my deepest, humblest, and heartfelt Infinite Love & Gratitude, thank you, Jeri Love! Thank you for your daily dedication, persistence, and passion to pray, work, and be world peace. Your mystical and magical creative alchemy transformed my intention, thoughts, and expression into this visionary book . . . thank you for your pure genius beyond compare. I love you and am so excited to be co-creating this tsunami wave of Infinite Love & Gratitude. Happy birthday every day! Everything is possible!

A special thanks to the LifeLine team, holding down home base in Northbrook, Illinois. Cindy Kaplan, you are the heart of it all . . . and I mean *it all!* You have an extraordinary way of bringing out the best in people and in the midst of chaos transforming life's experiences into a *butterfly.* Susan Isoe-Schneider, thank you for your unyielding presence and passion for spreading The LifeLine Technique. I'm so proud of you! As the Director of LifeLine

Technique Training Program, you're leading us to a whole new level. I'll forever remember, "One blade of grass . . ." Thank you, David Kaplan, my cousin, friend, and backbone of The LifeLine Technique trainings! Thank you, Ann Forowycz, my PR director, rock, and dear friend. Thank you for blessing me with your immense wisdom and extraordinary organization. A special thanks to Jenny Larson for sharing your design talents, creativity, and even more, your wonderful laugh. Thank you, Meredith Clark, for being a part of our research team. Welcome and thank you, Angie McDermott. You make a huge difference! Thank you for your unprecedented skills as an elite trainer and *leader!*

Very special thanks to Madge Bares. All I have to do is close my eyes and I'm there in the field. My heart is alive and forever grateful for your courage, trust, but mostly your friendship. Thanks to my dear friend Dr. Dan Ohlman (Dohlman). From Vegas to Tampa to Calgary (with the perfect view) to Long Beach . . . the journey is what it is because you're a part of it. I am forever blessed with the gift of your brotherhood. Thank you, Shawn Gallaway, for your musical spirit, shining heart, and peaceful soul. You are a true master. A heartfelt thank you to Mary Beth Shannon for being the beauty and passion beyond the words. Can you believe . . . ?

Thank you, Dr. Tom Bayne . . . the redwood has always lived within you. Thank you, Lauren Bondy, for shining the constellation of your soul!

Thank you to the "Queen Bee" of The Way to Optimal Health, Tammy Lavitt. You, my love, are a sacred gift from heaven. Thank you for supporting me to create *balance* in all of the spaces and places of my life . . . especially my heart! I'm so appreciative.

Thank you, Dr. Cari Jacobson! This is just the beginning of a magical mystery tour. Thank you for the greatest gift of your friendship. I am forever grateful! You are such a rock star . . . BAM!!!

Thank you to all of the Certified LifeLine Practitioners. I am so honored to have the most brilliant, compassionate, and powerful practitioners and friends on the planet. Your choice to connect with each other in a strong, loving, and real way humbles me . . .

it's almost as if there's an unspoken sacred contract that CLPs share, uniting us with intention to be the very best that we can be. Thank you from the depths of my heart for choosing to go for it.

Thank you, Ruth Bender! Once again, this book would not be what it is if it weren't for your eagle eye and discerning heart. Your editing skills are only paralleled by your soul's power to shine! I'm deeply grateful for our friendship.

Thank you, Bob Sandidge and Anne Ward! The new LifeLine Technique Flow Chart is beautiful, as are the wonderful graphics you did for this book. Our journey to Virginia Beach to speak at the A.R.E. and Sacramento to study with Kris and Tim Hallbom will forever live in my heart.

Thank you so much to Robin and Jerry Minor for having Source Books as a part of The LifeLine Technique trainings. You're both so beautiful, and I'm excited to continue to share the journey of life of friendship education through love, and loving through education.

Thank you to David Schiffman and Jeffrey Sofferman for being my best friends. What else can I say but it's a great life!

Thank you to Diane Mathews McCann and Robert McCann for being my family away from home. Beautiful Goddess Diane, you dropped into my life and shook it up! I'm so excited to spread The LifeLine Technique throughout Australia with you!

Thank you, Colette Baron-Reid and Marc Lindeman. I love you guys so much! Your friendship is one of my greatest treasures! Thank you, my sister Colette, for holding a sacred space for me to be whole.

Thank you, my friend Carla Johnston, for awakening The Truth!

Thank you to my Hay House family for being the wind beneath my wings. Louise Hay, I'm forever grateful to you for giving me the opportunity to soar! Thank you, Reid Tracy, for the opportunity to share this knowledge with the world. Your guidance along the journey has been immeasurable. Thank you, Jill Kramer, for your editorial expertise, your beautiful and kind heart, and the opportunity hopefully to play you in tennis someday. Thank you,

Alex Freemon, for helping to forge my life's passion into a work of art! Thank you, Christy Salinas and Jami Goddess, for the book's cover and design. Its essence expresses the power of Infinite Love & Gratitude! Thank you, Adrian Sandoval, for always rolling out the red carpet at the I Can Do It's for the LifeLine team! You are simply the best! Thank you, Donna Abate, for giving me my first tour of Hay House—I'll never forget it! Thank you, Diane Ray and Summer McStravick, for doing such a stand-up job with Hay House Radio . . . you and your team are superstars! Finally thank you so much, Nancy Levin and Chris Rauchnot, for your bright smiles and unwavering support. Nancy, your gentle yet powerful way brings peace and calm to all you come in contact with. Thank you for your great leadership.

Thank you to my family! From aunts and uncles to cousins and in-laws . . . you are my LifeLine. Thank you, Kenny, Paula, Howie, and Nicole Weissman. I appreciate and love you so much! To Mom and Dad, as you continue to celebrate your 50th wedding anniversary, I acknowledge you both for being two of my greatest teachers on the planet. I'm so blessed and deeply grateful for your presence in my life. Enjoy the next 50! I love you!

Meow to Zenny.

To my beloved and beautiful Sarit, thank you for sharing your sacred heart. You're my soul's most extraordinary manifestation! Our love is an eternal expression of two hearts dancing in the infinite botanical garden of oneness. Thank you for always being unconditionally supportive, constructive, and compassionate. And when you're not, thank you for being *you!* Our beautiful children send me over the top with a feeling that I can only describe as "Sapiola!" You're an amazing mother and wife, and yet it all stems from your commitment to being your best you! Life is ours to be shared and celebrated. May you always know how deeply I'm moved by the subtle expression of your smile. Forever falling in love.

Joya, Rumi, and Liam . . . thank you for the eternal soul reconnection. Your mommy and I love you soooooo much! I see you living in a peaceful world of love and compassion, filled with

Infinite Love & Gratitude. We will always do our best to share the simple truths of love. We hold you as a sacred expression of the divine spark. Thank you for teaching me . . . life is a miracle.

⊕⊕⊕ ⊕⊕⊕

About the Author

Dr. Darren R. Weissman, a Chicago native, is an internationally renowned physician, speaker, and educator; the developer of The LifeLine Technique™; and the best-selling author of *The Power of Infinite Love & Gratitude: An Evolutionary Journey to Awakening Your Spirit.* Darren is a contributing author for the best-selling book by Dr. Masaru Emoto *The Healing Power of Water.* He can also be seen in the films *Beyond Belief* and *The Truth.*

Darren has practiced holistic medicine for 15 years. As a speaker, he participates in conferences worldwide. He is a regular presenter at the Hay House "I Can Do It!" conference and "Celebrate Your Life!" conference by Mishka Productions. In addition, Darren teaches The LifeLine Technique™ in trainings around the world to participants from all backgrounds.

Darren earned his bachelor of science degree in human biology at the University of Kansas and his doctor of chiropractic medicine at the National College of Chiropractic. His postgraduate studies have included Applied Kinesiology (AK), Total Body Modification (TBM), Neuro Emotional Technique (NET), Neuro-Linguistic Programming (NLP), NeuroModulation Technique (NMT), Chinese energetic medicine, and natural healing. He has also had intensive holistic training in acupuncture and the Five Element Theory, Ayurveda and the chakras, shamanism, homeopathy, and magnet therapy, along with other forms of energy medicine, at the Kalubowila hospital in Colombo, Sri Lanka.

⊕⊕⊕ ⊕⊕⊕

Hay House Titles of Related Interest

YOU CAN HEAL YOUR LIFE, the movie,
starring Louise L. Hay & Friends
(available as a 1-DVD program and an expanded 2-DVD set)
Watch the trailer at: **www.LouiseHayMovie.com**

THE SHIFT, the movie, starring Dr. Wayne W. Dyer
(available as a 1-DVD program and an expanded 2-DVD set)
Watch the trailer at: **www.DyerMovie.com**

⊕ ⊕ ⊕

DEFY GRAVITY: Healing Beyond the Bounds of Reason,
by Caroline Myss

THE DIVINE NAME: The Sound That Can Change the World,
by Jonathan Goldman

EVERYTHING YOU NEED TO KNOW TO FEEL GO(O)D,
by Candace B. Pert, Ph.D., with Nancy Marriott

*FINDING OUR WAY HOME: Heartwarming Stories That Ignite Our
Spiritual Core,* by Gerald Jampolsky, M.D., and Diane Cirincione, Ph.D.

FRACTAL TIME: The Secret of 2012 and a New World Age,
by Gregg Braden

LIVING THROUGH THE RACKET:
How I Survived Leukemia . . . and Rediscovered
My Self, by Corina Morariu, with Allen Rucker

SANCTUARY: The Path of Consciousness,
by Stephen Lewis and Evan Slawson

SPONTANEOUS EVOLUTION: Our Positive
Future (and a Way to Get There from Here),
by Bruce H. Lipton, Ph.D., and Steve Bhaerman

SUPERCHARGED TAOIST: An Amazing True Story to Inspire
You on Your Own Adventure, by The Barefoot Doctor

THE THREE SISTERS OF THE TAO: Essential Conversations
with Chinese Medicine, I Ching, and Feng Shui,
by Terah Kathryn Collins (available June 2010)

TRAVELING AT THE SPEED OF LOVE, by Sonia Choquette

All of the above are available at your local bookstore,
or may be ordered by contacting Hay House (see next page).

⊕ ⊕ ⊕

We hope you enjoyed this Hay House book. If you'd like
to receive our online catalog featuring additional information
on Hay House books and products, or if you'd like to find
out more about the Hay Foundation, please contact:

Hay House, Inc., P.O. Box 5100, Carlsbad, CA 92018-5100

(760) 431-7695 or **(800) 654-5126**
(760) 431-6948 (fax) or **(800) 650-5115 (fax)**
www.hayhouse.com® • **www.hayfoundation.org**

⊕ ⊕ ⊕

Published and distributed in Australia by: Hay House Australia Pty.
Ltd., 18/36 Ralph St., Alexandria NSW 2015 • *Phone:* 612-9669-4299 •
Fax: 612-9669-4144 • www.hayhouse.com.au

Published and distributed in the United Kingdom by: Hay House
UK, Ltd., 292B Kensal Rd., London W10 5BE • *Phone:* 44-20-8962-1230 •
Fax: 44-20-8962-1239 • www.hayhouse.co.uk

Published and distributed in the Republic of South Africa by: Hay
House SA (Pty), Ltd., P.O. Box 990, Witkoppen 2068 • *Phone/Fax:*
27-11-467-8904 • info@hayhouse.co.za • www.hayhouse.co.za

Published in India by: Hay House Publishers India, Muskaan
Complex, Plot No. 3, B-2, Vasant Kunj, New Delhi 110 070 •
Phone: 91-11-4176-1620 • *Fax:* 91-11-4176-1630 • www.hayhouse.co.in

Distributed in Canada by: Raincoast, 9050 Shaughnessy St.,
Vancouver, B.C. V6P 6E5 • *Phone:* (604) 323-7100 •
Fax: (604) 323-2600 • www.raincoast.com

⊕ ⊕ ⊕

Take Your Soul on a Vacation

Visit **www.HealYourLife.com®** to regroup, recharge, and reconnect
with your own magnificence. Featuring blogs, mind-body-spirit news,
and life-changing wisdom from Louise Hay and friends.

Visit **www.HealYourLife.com** today!